ED YOUNG

THE TABLE

CASTING THE VISION
FOR THE LOCAL CHURCH

THE TABLE

SMALL GROUP STUDIES

Published in Dallas, TX by Creality Publishing.

All Scripture quotations, unless otherwise noted, are taken from The Holy Bible, New
International Version (North American Edition), copyright © 1973, 1978, 1984 by the
International Bible Society. Used by permission of Zondervan Publishing House.

Any emphases or parenthetical comments within Scripture are the author's own.

ISBN 0-9725813-4-0

CONTENTS

Small Groups are a vital part of how we do ministry at Fellowship Church just as they are in many churches around the world. There are a number of different theories on how small groups should work and they are all great in different ways. The book you are holding is written with our model in mind. So take a minute to read the following explanation, then feel free to adapt as necessary.

Each of our small groups practices a three part agenda in every meeting. That agenda includes a social time, a discussion time, and a prayer time. Each of these elements share equal importance, but not necessarily equal time. To help you get the most out of this book we have included an explanation of each of the parts.

The first element of every small group meeting should be a time of socializing. This phase of the meeting should about 30% of your time together. Welcome everyone as they arrive at the host home, make visitors feel welcome by introducing yourself and showing genuine interest in them. Enjoy some snacks, or if your group prefers, a meal together. Then move on with second part of the meeting, the lesson.

The lesson itself may take as much as 50% of your group's meeting time, but remember it is not the most important element. You may want to start this phase of your meeting with a short "icebreaker" to get everyone talking. The questions in the "Start it Up" section of each chapter are what we refer to as "level the playing field" questions that everyone should be able to participate in, regardless of their level of spiritual maturity or Bible knowledge. As your group moves through the "Talk it Up" section in each chapter, remember that it is more important to finish on time than to finish each and every question. It is okay to skip some to be sure you allow enough time to take care of the third phase of the small group time: "Lift it Up."

The "Lift it Up" section is a vital part of every small group meeting and should be about 20% of the meeting. During this time you will be able to share with the group what God is doing in your life as well as asking the group to support you in specific prayers. To help focus this time there are one or two questions at the end of each study that will prompt prayers based on the material you have just talked about. There is also a space for you to write down your prayer request(s) so you don't forget them and so you can communicate them clearly when it is your turn. Below that is a place to write down the prayer requests of the people in your group so you can remember and pray for each request throughout the week.

As an additional tool to assist you in your journey of spiritual development there is a "Step it Up" section at the end of each session. This section consists of five devotional thoughts that reinforce the lesson you've just completed and are designed to help you develop a regular quiet time with God. To get the absolute most from this study I challenge you to take five or ten minutes a day to read and apply these devotionals to your life. If your group meets twice a month or bi-weekly, choose five of the intervening days to incorporate these thoughts into your devotional life.

THE TABLE

One summer my wife and I took a day trip to the world's largest flea market in a little town called Canton, Texas. It was a trip that is hard to describe. I watched in amazement as thousands of shopping fanatics frantically pushed their shopping carts from shop to shop trying to find the deal of a lifetime. It was like sitting on the front row at some obscure Olympic competition.

After two or three longs hours on the quest for the ultimate flea market find, Lisa was gracious enough to say, "Honey, let's break for some lunch." Grateful for the reprieve, I accepted her offer and we headed off for the food court.

We bought a couple of chicken sandwiches and sat down to eat at one of the tables. After a few minutes, Lisa looked over my shoulder and said, "Ed, look!" I expected her to point out a rare piece of art or a bargain that we had somehow missed. But as I turned around, I noticed an employee of the restaurant carrying a tray of samples. Normally, a restaurant would hand out samples to potential customers. But this girl was weaving in and out of the picnic tables handing out samples to those of us who were already stuffing our faces with these same chicken sandwiches!

Lisa said, "That's hilarious. I mean, all she has to do is walk out about fifteen feet and offer the samples to people who haven't eaten yet." But she was obviously content to feed the already fed.

And that's when it hit me. I said, "Lisa, that's it! That is the local church in a nutshell."

The church has the greatest meal out there. Jesus said in John 6:35, "'I am the bread of life. He who comes to me will never go hungry and he who believes in me will never be thirsty again.'"

But for far too long we've been content weaving in and out of the church aisles handing out samples to the already fed, and we have missed the countless opportunities to offer the bread of life to a lost and dying world.

Christ is the ultimate carbohydrate, the only One capable of satisfying the deep spiritual hunger and thirst we all experience. And over the next twelve weeks, we're going to learn just how to present that meal, the bread of life, in ways that will attract others to "The Table."

This is hard-hitting stuff. I'm not going to pull any punches. But by creatively and intentionally reaching out to feed others the ultimate carbohydrate, you will also discover that your own spiritual hunger is satisfied by Christ.

INTRODUCTION

THE TABLE

START IT UP

When was the last time you bit into a perfectly flavored, cooked to perfection, choice cut of meat? When was the last time you sampled a dessert that was the perfect balance of each ingredient, culminating in an intense taste experience? Is your mouth starting to water as you remember the texture and flavor?

The food is important, but it takes more than just a prime recipe to make a memorable dining experience. Along with the right food, you must have the right environment. The environment might be an open field with a setting sun in the background, or a dimly lit table in the cozy corner of a café. The environment is essential in the ultimate dining experience. And what about the guest list? The perfect food and environment can be quickly ruined by the wrong guests.

As a group, dream up the ultimate dining experience. What food, environment and guest list would create an over-the-top dining dream?

This exercise might pique your interest about the ultimate dining dream. But is it just that: a dream? Does such an experience really exist? This series explores that question by examining the ultimate dining experience as designed by God. God desires to feed everyone with his dining design, and the best part is that you play a crucial role.

TALK IT UP

Did you know God designed the ultimate dining experience? God considered your needs, as well as the obstacles of the real life, and came up with the perfect solution. The food of this meal brings satisfaction like no other. The environment is carefully crafted to provide just the right elements to entice and engage every audience. The guest list is diverse and interesting, bringing a mix of people from all social situations. Best yet, you are personally invited to this dining experience, and you can bring as many guests with you as you wish.

By now you must be at least a little curious about this dining experience. After all, this experience was designed by the God who knows you more deeply and intimately than anyone else. He knows the secret needs of your heart—the ones you don't even realize you have.

Describe how has God satisfied a specific need in your life?

_____

_____

_____

_____

God wants to continue satisfying specific needs in your life and in the lives of those around you. And it all starts with the ultimate meal that provides satisfaction for all.

THE MEAL

The heart of Dallas' music scene is an area called Deep Ellum. It is an artsy, cool, hip place. And Deep Ellum is home to an incredible restaurant called The Green Room. It is unique, with eclectic art work and a strange ambiance—strange in a good way. The menu is not thick, but the food is four-star quality. The Green Room owners know that to be successful, you don't need to offer a huge variety; you just need to serve the food with excellence and creativity.

God's ultimate dining experience is the same way. He doesn't serve us a variety of different items half-heartedly; He just serves the right thing in the perfect way... the bread of life.

Read John 6:35

Why do you think Jesus described himself as the bread of life?

_____

_____

_____

_____

If you have made a decision to follow Christ, how has his food satisfied hungers in your life that were not satisfied before?

_____

_____

_____

_____

What do you think are some obstacles standing in the way of more people tasting the bread of life?

_____

_____

_____

God knew there would be some major obstacles in the way of getting this meal to all his creation. Because of this, he designed the ultimate place to serve the bread of life—an environment that would welcome anyone hungering for a satisfaction that will not fade.

THE TABLE

God knew when the word got out about the ultimate food, there would be millions wanting to taste this cosmic carbohydrate. God's perfect environment, his "Table," is not limited by a particular place. The Table translates into every culture and class of people. The idea behind it is simple, but the possibilities are endless.

The Table represents the local church. It has a divine design that allows the bread of life to be displayed in a way that others will be drawn. The Table is open, so space is not limited. The brilliance of the Table can be seen in its two-fold purpose: to serve seekers and nourish believers.

How have you seen Fellowship accomplishing the two-fold purpose of serving seekers and building believers at the Table?

_____

_____

_____

At the Table, the pastor is the dude with the food. He serves up the bread of life. But all those at the Table are not just waiting for the food. In God's design, it is the job of everyone to help serve the meal at his Table.

Read 1 John 3:1

Based on these verses and others in the New Testament, the message is that anyone who believes in Jesus is part of the family. We see that the Christ-followers are responsible for not only eating at the Table, but serving as well.

What are some ways that Christ-followers serve at the Table each week?

_____

_____

_____

Now that the meal and the environment have been mentioned, there is only one component left.

THE GUEST LIST

The right guest list is crucial to the ultimate meal. The interesting thing is that the guest list really depends on the purpose of the occasion. For example, a formal dinner followed by a night at the opera may be an enjoyable evening for some people. And ordering pizza and watching a movie on a big screen TV might be more to the liking of others.

Remember the two-fold purpose of the Table: to serve seekers and to build believers. Based on the purpose of the Table, describe what the guest list of the Table should look like.

_____

_____

_____

_____

_____

God's invitation to the Table is for everyone. God wants a diverse guest list at the Table. In fact, a healthy Table will consist of thirds. One third will be mature believers who have believed in Christ and been growing for a while. One third will be baby believers who have recently accepted Christ and are beginning to grow. Finally, one third will be seekers who have not yet stepped across the line of faith in Christ.

How do the thirds at the Table help fulfill God's two-fold mission for his church of serving seekers and building believers?

_____

_____

LIFT IT UP

The ultimate dining experience is an incredible opportunity for all of us to enjoy. God has invited you to the Table to feast on the bread of life.

How does it make you feel to realize God has invited you to the ultimate dining experience?

_____

_____

_____

If you are new to the Table, it might be a little overwhelming to think the one and only God wants to dine with you. If you will keep coming to the Table, you will find the God who can overwhelm you can also make you feel right at home. If you are a Christ-follower, you have a responsibility beyond just eating at the Table. While the privilege to be at the Table is great, so is the responsibility for each family member around the Table. God wants you to fully understand what is going on at the Table so that you can participate in the excitement of everything He has to offer in the ultimate dining experience.

Prayer Requests:

_____

_____

_____

_____

_____

_____

Notes:

_____

_____

_____

_____

_____

_____

_____

_____

_____

_____

_____

_____

_____

_____

_____

_____

_____

_____

STEP IT UP

Take a step further over the next few days and spend some time reflecting on the following devotional thoughts that reinforce the previous session. Use these as reminders to take what you've learned and apply it to your everyday life.

DAY 1

How great is the love the Father has lavished on us, that we should be called children of God! And that is what we are! The reason the world does not know us is that it did not know him. -- 1 John 3:1

Do you remember the story of Annie? She is the little red headed orphan that desperately desires a family. She lives in an orphanage of abuse and neglect when Daddy Warbucks rescues her. Daddy Warbucks is a rich bachelor with a home and possessions beyond Annie's imagination. By the end of the story, Annie has the family she has always imagined and riches beyond her wildest dream.

There is a little bit of Annie in all of us. Every person has the desire to belong to something similar to a family. The desire to be loved and to have a unique bond with a group of individuals is in every one. God knows that desire and has answered it in the form of a relationship with him. God is the ultimate Daddy Warbucks with riches beyond compare and a love that is unrivaled. When you accept a relationship with him through Jesus, you instantly become a part of the family.

Being in God's family is an experience without equal. There are not the dysfunctions of so many other families. Holiday celebrations are not accompanied by the usual moments of misery present in so many other families. Have you stopped to consider how good it is to be a part of the family of God?

Spend time considering the greatness of being in God's family. Thank him for opportunity he has given you. Ask for wisdom in how to represent the family well.

Notes:

_____

_____

_____

_____

_____

_____

_____

_____

Prayer Requests:

_____

_____

_____

_____

_____

_____

_____

_____

_____

DAY 2

They all ate and were satisfied, -- Mark 6:42

Think back to the last time you were truly hungry. It is a unique feeling of emptiness and desire. It can be frustrating at times, and debilitating in extreme circumstances. The gnawing of a hungry stomach can easily distract you from the moment and shift your focus. On the other hand, the feeling of a full stomach is a great feeling after you have experienced hunger. Not the feeling of an overstuffed stomach, but that feeling of eating just the right amount of the right thing.

When Jesus fed the people, their hunger changed to a feeling of satisfaction. What Jesus did with a few loaves of bread and a couple fish thousands of years ago is still happening today. He is not dividing the crowds into groups and having them once again sit in the grassy field. He is not stuck simply satisfying stomachs. Jesus is satisfying some of the most intense hungers known to man.

The hunger for love is being fed by Jesus' ultimate act of love. The hunger for a healthy self-esteem is being satisfied as people find their purpose and value in Christ. The hunger for direction in life is quenched. Hunger after hunger is brought to Jesus and he meets them. He will continue to do this for all who come to him.

How has God satisfied your hungers of the past? Have you brought your hungers to God lately? What hunger do you need to allow God to satisfy?

Notes:

_____

_____

_____

_____

_____

_____

_____

_____

_____

Prayer Requests:

_____

_____

_____

_____

_____

_____

_____

_____

_____

DAY 3

Isaac spoke up and said to his father Abraham, "Father?" "Yes, my son?" Abraham replied. "The fire and wood are here," Isaac said, "but where is the lamb for the burnt offering?" Abraham answered, "God himself will provide the lamb for the burnt offering, my son." And the two of them went on together. -- Genesis 22:7-8

God promised and Abraham waited... and waited. God promised Abraham a family that would become a great nation. This nation would be God's people and represent God to the world. The nations would be blessed through the offspring of Abraham. All of this was incredible except for one thing, Abraham had no children.

Abraham waited on God to provide the child that would lead to the fulfillment of God's promise. Finally, God provided Abraham with a son named Isaac. All the waiting had been worth it. All the doubt was removed. The answer to so many questions was now walking with Abraham to answer one of the greatest questions of Abraham's life. Would Abraham trust God?

God told Abraham to sacrifice his son, the son that was waited for, the fulfillment of God's promise. God was not asking for another $10 in the offering plate. God was asking for Abraham's son. Abraham was on his way to give God his son. Isaac's question about the lamb for the burnt offering has new meaning in light of what was going on.

Abraham's trust also has new meaning. Abraham trusted God to provide... and God did. Do you trust God to provide for your needs? Do you allow God to have control of providing for you even when it is hard... really hard... Abraham and Isaac hard?

Consider your needs. Do you trust God to provide for you?

Notes:

_____

_____

_____

_____

_____

_____

_____

_____

_____

Prayer Requests:

_____

_____

_____

_____

_____

_____

_____

_____

_____

DAY 4

*Now a man came up to Jesus and asked, "Teacher, what good thing must I do to get eternal life?" "Why do you ask me about what is good?" Jesus replied. "There is only One who is good. If you want to enter life, obey the commandments." "Which ones?" the man inquired. Jesus replied, " 'Do not murder, do not commit adultery, do not steal, do not give false testimony, honor your father and mother,' and 'love your neighbor as yourself.'" "All these I have kept," the young man said. "What do I still lack?" Jesus answered, "If you want to be perfect, go, sell your possessions and give to the poor, and you will have treasure in heaven. Then come, follow me." When the young man heard this, he went away sad, because he had great wealth.
-- Matthew 19:16-22*

"So close yet so far away" is an accurate phrase for this story. The man had tracked down Jesus and was now standing close enough to see him. He got the opportunity to have a conversation with the Son of God. This man was standing within feet of Jesus. As close as the man got to Jesus, it was not close enough. There was an obstacle between the man and Jesus that proximity could not cross.

The man was wealthy. His piles of plush possessions became an obstacle in a relationship with Jesus. The man could not get over his possessions. Jesus stood on one side and the man stood on the other side refusing to cross over to Jesus. This still happens today. Some people stand behind the obstacle of their own pride. Others stand behind the obstacle of bad church experiences. Obstacles come in many shapes and sizes. All of them can be dangerous if not dealt with.

What do you think are common obstacles that keep more of your friends from having a relationship with God? What could you do to help you friends overcome those obstacles?

Notes:

_____

_____

_____

_____

_____

_____

_____

_____

_____

Prayer Requests:

_____

_____

_____

_____

_____

_____

_____

_____

_____

DAY 5

Jesus spoke to them again in parables, saying: "The kingdom of heaven is like a king who prepared a wedding banquet for his son. He sent his servants to those who had been invited to the banquet to tell them to come, but they refused to come. "Then he sent some more servants and said, 'Tell those who have been invited that I have prepared my dinner: My oxen and fattened cattle have been butchered, and everything is ready. Come to the wedding banquet.' "But they paid no attention and went off—one to his field, another to his business. The rest seized his servants, mistreated them and killed them. The king was enraged. He sent his army and destroyed those murderers and burned their city. "Then he said to his servants, 'The wedding banquet is ready, but those I invited did not deserve to come. Go to the street corners and invite to the banquet anyone you find.' So the servants went out into the streets and gathered all the people they could find, both good and bad, and the wedding hall was filled with guests. -- Matthew 22:1-8

There is a popular show on television where extravagant parties are thrown in honor of particular teenagers. These teenagers are allowed to invite whomever they desire to their parties. Invitations to these parties quickly become coveted prizes due to the exclusivity of the event. There are hurt feelings, angry attitudes and dishonest counterfeiting happening at the door as individuals vie for a place in the party.

Some churches share characteristics with those teenage parties. The church is a big event where only the popular are invited. Many desire to come to church, but there is a feeling of exclusivity. The problem is the church was never intended to be exclusive. The parable told by Jesus emphasizes God's desire to be inclusive rather than exclusive. The members of the church play a significant role in this. While we communicate that Christ is the only way to heaven, we also welcome people from all backgrounds into the doors of the church to hear his message of hope and forgiveness.

Are you including others in your church? How does your lifestyle answer this question? What do your words communicate about your efforts to include others in the church?

Notes:

_____

_____

_____

_____

_____

_____

_____

_____

_____

Prayer Requests:

_____

_____

_____

_____

_____

_____

_____

_____

_____

WHAT'S COOKING? - PART 1

THE TABLE

START IT UP

Last time, we discussed how God has designed the ultimate dining experience. In that experience there are three key elements. One element is the church—the Table where people go to get fed the truth of the Bible. The two-fold purpose of the Table is to serve seekers and build believers.

This purpose is reflected in another element of the dining experience, the guest list. The guest list should represent the thirds: one-third mature believers, one-third baby believers and one-third seekers. And the final element is the food God serves at the Table—the bread of life.

What is your favorite food? Forget about nutrition, vitamins, and protein as you answer this next question. If you could only eat one food for the next thirty days, what would you choose?

Now, for this next part of the question, think about all the nutrients you need to be healthy. Is there any food you think you could eat for thirty days without getting sick?

It would take a very special food to be able to eat it for thirty days straight without getting tired of it and without getting sick. Imagine how special the food would have to be to eat the same food for a year straight and not get sick and tired of it! This might sound impossible, but God has an incredible way of making the impossible possible.

TALK IT UP

God provided a long-term creative cuisine for his people twice in history. The first example happened almost 1500 years before Jesus walked the earth. God had just freed his people after 400 years of living in slavery in another land. God orchestrated their escape from Egyptian bondage through one of the most famous figures in Old Testament history... Moses.

For those of you who know the story, in your own words describe what God did through Moses to free his people.

_____

_____

The people saw God do something incredible for them as they began their journey to the Promised Land. And yet, their gratefulness did not last long. In a short time, they were complaining about the same God who just answered their prayers and freed them from slavery.

THE HUNGER

Read Exodus 16:2-3

The people got hungry, and their hunger changed their perspective of God. They quickly forgot how God provided for them by freeing them from slavery, parting the Red Sea so they could cross, and guiding them with a pillar of cloud and fire. Their hunger blinded them.

How has a hunger in your life caused you to complain and forget how God has provided for you?

_____

_____

_____

If you are unsatisfied, God already knows. He is waiting for you to come to him with your lack of satisfaction. But, do not forget all God has done for you in the past just because you currently feel unsatisfied. God is so generous that sometimes even when His children ask without being thankful and grateful, he still provides for them.

MANNA MEAL

Read Exodus 16:6-8, 13-16

God provided the perfect food for the Israelites. Remember, at the beginning of this discussion, you tried to think of a food you could eat for thirty days without getting sick. God designed a food the Israelites could eat for forty years without getting sick! Manna was specifically designed by God to provide for all the Israelites' nutritional needs. God provided for them, despite their asking without being thankful.

How has God provided for you even when you asked with the wrong attitude or maybe the wrong motives? What did you learn from that situation?

_____

_____

_____

In an incredible act, God provided his people with a creative cuisine that met all their needs. Imagine getting up every morning and walking out your front door to find your food for the day sitting on your doorstep. God gave his people a daily reminder of his power and provision.

What things does God use to remind you on a regular basis on his power and provision?

_____

_____

_____

Despite the manna meal, the people did not trust God enough to follow his plan. They had specific instructions to only take what they needed for the day. Otherwise, it would rot. Even with the knowledge of God's perfect plan for their manna meal, some chose a different meal plan and suffered the consequences.

MANNA MENTALITY

Read Exodus 16:19-20

Discuss a time that God provided you with a great gift that you did not use according to his plan. In your experience, what happens to God's provision when you use it apart from his plan?

_____

_____

_____

There are all sorts of temptations out there that try to get us to stray from God's plan for our lives. God has a perfect plan to provide for you on a daily basis, but it takes choosing to eat what he has provided in the way he commands. Many times we get the manna mentality and take God's provisions apart from his plan. It might be taking the money God provides for you through your job and not being faithful to give back God's portion. Maybe you have a relationship God provided, but you are not following his plan in that relationship. The manna mentality can creep in if you are not careful.

What provisions seem to be the easiest to get the manna mentality with? What has helped you overcome the manna mentality?

_____

_____

_____

LIFT IT UP

God provided a satisfying, creative cuisine for his people 1500 years before Christ, the ultimate bread of life ever walked the earth. God is such a generous provider, but sometimes we forget about his provision and choose our own plans. The last part of this lesson is an opportunity to refocus on how God has provided for you.

Spend the next 5 minutes taking turns sharing with the group the thing that God has provided for you that makes you the most thankful.

God provided for his people in the desert during the time of Moses, but the provision did not stop there. Next week we will take a look at the first combo meal deal in history. On top of that, we will get to discover God's ultimate in creative cuisine.

Prayer Requests:

_____

_____

_____

_____

_____

_____

_____

_____

_____

STEP IT UP

Take a step further over the next few days and spend some time reflecting on the following devotional thoughts that reinforce the previous session. Use these as reminders to take what you've learned and apply it to your everyday life.

DAY 1

In the desert the whole community grumbled against Moses and Aaron. The Israelites said to them, "If only we had died by the LORD's hand in Egypt! There we sat around pots of meat and ate all the food we wanted, but you have brought us out into this desert to starve this entire assembly to death." -- Exodus 16:2-3

Have you ever been attacked by the "good ol' days" syndrome? It's when you think back to a particular time in your life and your memory erases all the bad and emphasizes the good. A lot of times the "good ol' days" syndrome can attack when you are going through a difficult situation and you want a way out.

That is what happened to the Israelites. God rescued them and was leading them to a promising land of provision, but they started complaining. They started reminiscing about their days in Egypt. They completely forgot their slavery and starvation. They ignored everything God was currently giving them, and wished for the past. They actually thought they were better off in slavery!

Before you call the Israelites crazy, think about your life. Has there ever been a time you suffered from the "good ol' days" syndrome? You might be in the middle of a difficult situation, so you think about something you had to give up in order to follow God's plan. You forget about the negative aspects of that situation and only focus on the positive. And before you know it, you are wishing for those "good ol' days."

Do not fall for it. God's provision is always better than your past. God can give you clear vision about your situation. Weigh out God's provision versus your past and see what comes out on top. When you face the temptation to have the "good ol' days" syndrome, ask God to give you clear vision.

Notes:

_____

_____

_____

_____

_____

_____

_____

_____

_____

_____

Prayer Requests:

_____

_____

_____

_____

_____

_____

_____

_____

_____

_____

DAY 2

The LORD said to Moses, "I have heard the grumbling of the Israelites. Tell them, 'At twilight you will eat meat, and in the morning you will be filled with bread. Then you will know that I am the LORD your God.'"
-- Exodus 16:11-12

Have you ever received something you did not deserve? We all have. Maybe you treated a friend badly, and they were still nice to you. How about a time you complained about a situation and it turned out to be far better than you had expected?

God provided for the Israelites despite their grumbling and dissatisfaction about what he had given them. God provided his people with meat and bread called "manna." For the rest of Israel's journey in the desert, God provided them with food.

God's continuing provision is out there for you as well. Have you ever complained about God's provision even though he has given you great gifts? Ask God for forgiveness if you've been complaining, and thank him for providing for you even when you do not deserve it.

Notes:

_____

_____

_____

_____

_____

_____

_____

_____

_____

Prayer Requests:

_____

_____

_____

_____

_____

_____

_____

_____

_____

DAY 3

Then the LORD said to Moses, "I will rain down bread from heaven for you. The people are to go out each day and gather enough for that day. In this way I will test them and see whether they will follow my instructions. On the sixth day they are to prepare what they bring in, and that is to be twice as much as they gather on the other days." -- Exodus 16:4-5

God's provision for the Israelites came with a plan; just like his original provision for Adam and Eve came with a plan. Following God's plan for the provision is not only a way for you to experience the best blessing possible, but also it is a way for God to make sure you are in a right relationship with him. God wants to make sure your heart is with him. If you will not give him control of what he has given you, that shows him that your heart is not really with him.

Take time today to give God control of the provision he has given you is not a one day process. It takes time and daily decisions. Pray for God to help you start the process today.

Notes:

_____

_____

_____

_____

_____

_____

_____

_____

_____

Prayer Requests:

_____

_____

_____

_____

_____

_____

_____

_____

DAY 4

Then Moses said to them, "No one is to keep any of it until morning." However, some of them paid no attention to Moses; they kept part of it until morning, but it was full of maggots and began to smell. So Moses was angry with them. -- Exodus 16:19-20

There is a country song that says, "Too much of a good thing is a good thing." You might wonder How could that be true? If the small Blizzard® ice cream treat from Dairy Queen is good, then the large must be great, right? It is easy to overdose by piling on too much of a good thing. We've all done that before.

If you keep stuffing your face full of Blizzards, you will get sick. Your body can only handle so much ice cream at one time. God designed it that way. You were not designed to digest gallons at a time.

The same is true in other aspects of your life. God has designed you with limits, even for the good things in life. Many times, good things can be made into sinful things by pushing the limits.

Having a nice home and a nice car can be good things. But being consumed with these good things becomes sin when we live beyond our means. God gives us financial limits so that we honor him with the stuff he has entrusted to us. A relationship with a beautiful member of the opposite sex can be a good thing. But becoming consumed with that relationship and placing him or her before God is a bad thing. A boyfriend or a spouse is never meant to replace God. Unfortunately, seeking too much of a good thing can be easy to do.

Is there any area of your life where you are getting God's provision out of whack? What area are you pushing for too much of a good thing? Give it back to God, and ask him to help you with your portion control.

Notes:

_____

_____

_____

_____

_____

_____

_____

_____

_____

_____

Prayer Requests:

_____

_____

_____

_____

_____

_____

_____

_____

_____

_____

DAY 5

"Six days you are to gather it, but on the seventh day, the Sabbath, there will not be any." Nevertheless, some of the people went out on the seventh day to gather it, but they found none. Then the LORD said to Moses, "How long will you refuse to keep my commands and my instructions?" -- Exodus 16:26-28

God wants to provide for us in a fulfilling way. The problem is that many times our search for fulfillment tempts us to go outside of God's provision. Like the Israelites from the verses you read today, we search for fulfillment where God has not placed his provision. But it is very dangerous to wander away from God's provision in search of fulfillment.

Think about the last scary movie you saw. There is one common scene in every scary movie. It generally happens after at least one person has already been attacked. The prideful guy or girl in the group stands up and proclaims something to this effect, "You guys can keep this up, but I'm going my own way. Who's going with me?" That is generally a sure sign that character is about to make a speedy exit from the movie's script.

Don't be that prideful person who stands up to God and announces that you are going in your own direction. You will only discover the same emptiness the Israelites discovered when they rebelled. Examine yourself to discover if there is any area of your life where you are leaving God's provision. Ask God to forgive you and bring you back into his everlasting provision.

Notes:

_____

_____

_____

_____

_____

_____

_____

_____

_____

_____

Prayer Requests:

_____

_____

_____

_____

_____

_____

_____

_____

_____

WEEK THREE

WHAT'S COOKING? - PART 2

THE TABLE

START IT UP

Diets are in. From carb-free to protein-packed; from portion control to prepackaged, it seems everyone has a plan. Have you tried one of the popular diets? Describe your experiences with diets.

TALK IT UP

There are a lot of diets out there, and many of them are just fad diets. They may work for a while, but the results cannot be sustained. But God has designed a definitive diet that has been proven effective for 2000 years. It is a diet that God was preparing thousands of years ago when some the people who met Jesus face-to-face found themselves hungry in the middle of nowhere with nothing around to satisfy their hunger. It was here that Jesus fed over 5000 people the first Hebrew Happy Meal®.

THE HEBREW HAPPY MEAL

Read John 6:5-13

Jesus provided the people with a miraculous Hebrew Happy Meal. But he did not stop his perplexing provision years ago. He still provides for his people today in unexpected ways.

41

How has Jesus provided for you in an unexpected way? What was your response to that provision?

_____

_____

_____

Read on and discover how the people around Jesus responded to this Hebrew Happy Meal.

STILL HUNGRY

Read John 6:25-27

Miracles caused many people to follow Jesus, but that was not the case with this crowd. These people followed Jesus because he put food in their stomachs—he fulfilled a physical need. Miraculous signs still do not cause as many people to follow God as when he meets a personal need. Think back to a time that you saw a "miracle" happen on a Christian television program. Did it cause you to believe and follow? More often than miraculous signs, having our personal needs met causes us to follow God.

How have you seen somebody's perspective about God change because they had a personal need met?

_____

_____

_____

Our personal needs are powerful. Many people spend their entire lives trying to satisfy a personal need. There is the perfectionist who cannot leave one detail undone because she is still trying to win approval from others that they did not receive as a child. The obsessive compulsive might be trying to overcome an insecurity that developed from a failed relationship. The workaholic might be determined to provide the things for his family that he never had. Trying to satisfy a personal need is not a bad thing. The key is the way you go about finding that satisfaction.

How have you seen personal needs drive everything in someone's life or in your own experience?

_____

_____

_____

Jesus describes himself as the "Son of Man" and says that he can offer people a food that endures through eternal life. Jesus knows we have personal needs that need to be satisfied today. But he also knows we will never be satisfied until our spiritual hunger is satisfied. Only Jesus can satisfy the ultimate hunger of our spirit.

FINDING YOUR FILL

Read John 6:28-35

The people were curious about this satisfying bread that was better than the previous manna meal, so they asked how they could eat. Jesus explained that eating required believing in him—a belief that leads to sustained satisfaction.

If you are a Christ-follower, describe your first taste of the bread of life; in other words, describe your first encounter with Jesus. How old were you? How did it happen? How did you respond?

_____

_____

_____

Jesus promises fulfillment from eating the bread of life. Some of you have tasted the bread of life once and you expected to find satisfaction. Maybe you look at the bread of life as an afternoon snack. The bread of life is not a snack— it's a full meal deal! God serves only one food for satisfaction, so if you fill your stomach with anything else you will not find true satisfaction. You must feast on the bread of life every day and in every minute. But Satan wants you to cheat on your divine diet.

What snacks does Satan try to tempt you with the most? How has God helped you to overcome your cravings to snack?

_____

_____

_____

Others of you are not satisfied because you are just nibbling on the bread of life, little nibbles here and there. God wants you to take big bites. God wants you to taste and see how good life with him can be.

What are some practical things that you can do to make sure you are getting a healthy portion of the bread of life?

_____

_____

_____

LIFT IT UP

Finish tonight by evaluating how much you are dining on the bread of life. The amount you eat and the amount of satisfaction you experience are directly related. The following are some key questions to get you thinking about how to dine regularly on the bread of life. For every question, mark an "x" on the line closest to your answer for the question.

1. Which phrase best describes your attitude toward the church?

Who needs it	If there is nothing better	Pretty important	Foundation in my life

2. How well do you apply the lessons you learn both in the main service and at your small group?

In one ear	Think about it	Talk about it	Live it out

3. How often do you give your time to serve God?

He wants me?	I would like to but...	Learning to	Regular commitment

4. Describe your spiritual eating habits away from the church such as reading your Bible and praying.

I'm starving	I'm snacking	Finicky but faithful	Chair by the buffet

5. How well do you share your spiritual food with others?

All for me	Spare a crumb	Leftovers	Main course

The right side of the lines represents healthy eating habits. The more you marked on the right side of the lines, the more likely it is that you will experience the satisfaction we have discussed in this lesson. When it comes to dining on the bread of life, give up your mid-afternoon snacks and go for the full meal deal.

Prayer Requests:

_____

_____

_____

_____

_____

_____

STEP IT UP

Take a step further over the next few days and spend some time reflecting on the following devotional thoughts that reinforce the previous session. Use these as reminders to take what you've learned and apply it to your everyday life.

DAY 1

When Jesus looked up and saw a great crowd coming toward him, he said to Philip, "Where shall we buy bread for these people to eat?" He asked this only to test him, for he already had in mind what he was going to do. Philip answered him, "Eight months' wages would not buy enough bread for each one to have a bite!" Another of his disciples, Andrew, Simon Peter's brother, spoke up, "Here is a boy with five small barley loaves and two small fish, but how far will they go among so many?" -- John 6:5-9

Here you see another crowd with another hunger. Last time it was hungry Hebrews in the desert being fed by God. This time, it is Jesus designing a plan to provide food for them. By now, you are probably realizing God is in the catering business. The problem in this passage is the supply of food does not match the demand. There are at least 5000 hungry people ready to eat and the disciples do not have the resources or food to feed them all. All they come up with is five small loaves of bread and two fish.

What is your hunger? Are you starving for a new job? Is it the craving for a spouse? Are you feeling the hunger pains of wanting your family to function? As you evaluate your hunger, you might be looking at the resources you have to satisfy your hunger and feel helpless. You might feel like you have as much hope as feeding 5000 with five small loaves of bread and two fish.

Do not give up! Bring your hunger and your resources to Jesus. You can also bring your questions and doubts, because Jesus is big enough to handle them. The important thing is that you bring it all to Jesus and seek him for the satisfaction for your hunger. Examine your life and determine where you are hungry. Pray and ask God to take control of the situation and your resources.

Notes:

_____

_____

_____

_____

_____

_____

_____

_____

_____

Prayer Requests:

_____

_____

_____

_____

_____

_____

_____

_____

_____

DAY 2

Jesus said, "Have the people sit down." There was plenty of grass in that place, and the men sat down, about five thousand of them. Jesus then took the loaves, gave thanks, and distributed to those who were seated as much as they wanted. He did the same with the fish. When they had all had enough to eat, he said to his disciples, "Gather the pieces that are left over. Let nothing be wasted." So they gathered them and filled twelve baskets with the pieces of the five barley loaves left over by those who had eaten. -- John 6:10-13

What has happened since you brought your hunger to Jesus? Maybe you are reading this passage as a satisfied person. Maybe you are still hungry, but you have a new perspective on your hunger. Regardless of your condition, don't give up. Think about what you read today. Jesus more than satisfied the crowd. In fact, there were leftovers when he was finished.

I wonder how many people were following Jesus, looking for satisfaction that day, started to get hungry, but turned and left before they could see him work. If they would have just kept on with Jesus, there would have been more than enough left over for them. Who knows how many went away hungry simply because they let their hunger make them quit? Don't be one of those who walk away hungry. Jesus can satisfy you in an incredible way if you will stay with him.

Bring your hungers and resources to God. Offer them once again and ask for the strength to believe in him and watch as he provides for you.

THE TABLE

Notes:

_____

_____

_____

_____

_____

_____

_____

_____

_____

_____

Prayer Requests:

_____

_____

_____

_____

_____

_____

_____

_____

_____

_____

DAY 3

When they found him on the other side of the lake, they asked him, "Rabbi, when did you get here?" Jesus answered, "I tell you the truth, you are looking for me, not because you saw miraculous signs but because you ate the loaves and had your fill. Do not work for food that spoils, but for food that endures to eternal life, which the Son of Man will give you. On him God the Father has placed his seal of approval." -- John 6:25-27

Jesus' provision can be an incredible thing. Hurting hearts find healing in his presence. Limited finances can pay unlimited bills. Those with low self-esteem become highly esteemed before Jesus. The list can go on and on, as thousands upon thousands of hungers are met. Satisfaction is found by those who thought they would always hunger. In the midst of all these needs being met, don't miss out on the way Jesus can satisfy the ultimate hunger.

Jesus told those he had recently fed to look for food that endures. He was there to offer them satisfaction from a hunger that could never be filled in the natural world. Jesus knew fulfilling all the natural hungers in the world would never satisfy the masses unless their spiritual hunger was met.

Think about it for a second. If Jesus could feed over 5000 with five loaves and two fish, how hard would it be for him to wipe out hunger across the world if that was his goal? Jesus did not do it in his earthly ministry because he knew mankind had a much greater hunger.

Have you allowed Jesus to satisfy your spiritual hunger? Believe in him, and ask him to satisfy your spiritual hunger.

Notes:

_____

_____

_____

_____

_____

_____

_____

_____

_____

Prayer Requests:

_____

_____

_____

_____

_____

_____

_____

_____

DAY 4

Do not work for food that spoils, but for food that endures to eternal life, which the Son of Man will give you. On him God the Father has placed his seal of approval." -- John 6:27

It can be one of the most disturbing chores you do in a normal household. It generally happens when you run out of room to cram anything else into the limited space. It's the dreaded deed of cleaning out your refrigerator.

As you navigate the shelves and drawers, you come across Tupperware® containers of mystery. What smell will be revealed when you open the lid? How moldy will the food be inside the pastel colored bowl? If you survive the Tupperware containers, you still have plenty of plastic bags and Saran® wrapped wonders. And, if you are truly brave, you will explore the expiration dates on the condiments and other containers.

All of this is a reminder of an important biblical principle: ordinary food spoils. But it's not just food that has a limited shelf life. Money loses its value because of inflation. Cutting-edge fashion quickly becomes an exercise in what not to wear. Possessions depreciate and tarnish.

Spoiling is going on all around you this very minute. It is just a part of life and something you do not have to worry about unless all your investments are tied up in spoiling items. Think beyond your pocketbook for a minute when it comes to investments. Where are you investing your time? What has your heart's passion? Those are the most important things you can invest.

Jesus said, "Invest in what will always appreciate and endure." Jesus knew about investments that last beyond the close of Wall Street. He knew satisfaction could only come from investing your heart in God's principles and promises. This means buying in fully to God's plan. It is the one investment you can make that will always appreciate and endure.

Evaluate your investments honestly. What are the top 5 things that get your heart and time?

THE TABLE WHAT'S COOKING? - PART 2

Notes:

Prayer Requests:

DAY 5

Then Jesus declared, "I am the bread of life. He who comes to me will never go hungry, and he who believes in me will never be thirsty."
-- John 6:35

What is comfort to you? For some it is the solace of a half gallon of double chocolate ice cream. Comfort can be in the crowded atmosphere of a concert or sporting event. Is it good friends or mom's home cooking?

Comfort comes in many different forms. But the problem of comfort is that it is conditional. All these things provide comfort for a moment, but that moment is fleeting.

Jesus, on the other hand, has come to provide limitless satisfaction. Jesus is the true bread of life, and any person who eats of him will never go hungry or thirsty. Imagine satisfaction without limits. This doesn't mean that those who come to Jesus will never endure another hardship in life, but they will always have the way out, the truth to their questions and a life that will be fulfilled.

You've been challenged throughout this study to ask Jesus to satisfy your hunger. Is Jesus your ultimate source of satisfaction? Are you living out that belief today? Do you truly trust Jesus as the ultimate source for your satisfaction? Ask God to reveal to you any area where you may be searching for satisfaction apart from him.

THE TABLE WHAT'S COOKING? - PART 2

Notes:

_____

_____

_____

_____

_____

_____

_____

_____

_____

Prayer Requests:

_____

_____

_____

_____

_____

_____

_____

_____

WEEK FOUR

THE TWO-FOLD PURPOSE

THE TABLE

START IT UP

This series has been all about the ultimate dining experience provided by God. Over the past two lessons, you have examined how God provides a creative cuisine to satisfy his people. God's ultimate creative cuisine is the bread of life, Christ. By taking in the bread of life, you can find lasting satisfaction. The ultimate dining experience is served in a unique and purpose filled environment. Tonight begins your examination of the Table where God serves the bread of life.

Eating out is one of our favorite pastimes as Americans. Discuss the following questions related to different aspects of a dining experience at one of your favorite restaurants:

- *How often do you go out to eat? How does the service affect your enjoyment of the meal?*

- *How would you describe your favorite restaurant's "ambience"? What role does that play in where you decide to eat out?*

TALK IT UP

The church is a restaurant that serves the "Bread of Life" to hungry masses every week. The way the attendees, especially the visitors, are served when they come to the church can have a direct impact on their desire to come back for that bread again and again. Also, the members who volunteer in various capacities of the church contribute to its overall ambience.

Describe the first experience you can remember with church.

_____

_____

_____

In your opinion, what role does the attitudes of the volunteers and the "ambience" play in making people comfortable at church?

_____

_____

_____

Regardless of how familiar you may or may not be about the purpose of the church, talking about it is very important. That's why we've devoted an entire lesson to explore the two-fold purpose of the church, represented in this study by the Table.

THE PURPOSE

The Table's two-fold purpose is to build believers and serve seekers. Everything that happens at the Table should fit into one of the two parts of the purpose. The purpose was not just randomly chosen. This two-fold purpose is biblically grounded; it is fundamental to the nature of what the church was intended to be.

Read Ephesians 5:23

Identify the relationship of Christ and the church as described in Ephesians and come up with other metaphors to help define this relationship.

_____

_____

_____

_____

The church is uniquely connected to Christ. It was designed to be an extension of what Christ was about while on earth. The programs of every local church should reflect what is known about Christ. The things most important to Christ should be a primary concern at the Table.

Based on the devotionals from this past week, as well as other things you know about Christ, what are examples of how he built up those who believed in him? What are some examples of how Christ served those seeking him?

_____

_____

_____

_____

_____

The church's purpose is based on its head, Christ. So we follow Christ and strive to build believers and serve seekers because that is what Christ did. When people come to the Table, they deserve a quality presentation of the bread of life. The ultimate food deserves the ultimate presentation. This type of presentation requires keeping all the guests in mind (which will be discussed in the coming week), as well as balancing the purpose of building believers and serving seekers.

BALANCING ACT

A church that only builds believers primarily turns inward. Members of that church miss out on the incredible experience of being like Christ by serving those who are not believers.

Read Matthew 9:9-13

Christ made it abundantly clear that his focus was not just on believers. One moment he called Matthew to be a believer, and the next moment he made Matthew part of serving seekers. If Christ did this, the church empowered by God should do the same.

What were some of the things you were looking for as you were seeking Christ? What did the church offer that helped you find him?

_____

_____

_____

Just like being unbalanced towards building believers can be unhealthy, only serving seekers can also be unhealthy. The church must remember the dangers of becoming unbalanced.

What do you think could happen to a church if it was only about serving seekers?

_____

_____

_____

You know now that part of the purpose of the church is to build believers. Consider Christ's words to Peter when he invited Peter to, once again, be a part of his ministry.

Read John 21:15-17

Some of Christ's final words to Peter were all about building believers. Christ thought it was so important that he emphasized it by repeating it three times. If it was that important to Christ, it should be important to the church as well.

As a believer, what do you need to be built up? How has the local church met your needs and built you up?

_____

_____

_____

Sometimes believers complain because they feel their needs are not being met. Many times, the complaint comes from their focus being misplaced—they forget the two-fold purpose of the church. The church cannot just focus on building believers and providing believers with everything they feel they need. That would not be healthy.

What could be some of the problems with a church that only builds believers and neglects serving seekers?

_____

_____

_____

SERVING THE MEAL

The ultimate food deserves the ultimate presentation, and you play a crucial role in the presentation from two stand points.

First, those who are at the Table; those who are Christ followers, are responsible for serving the food. People form opinions about the meal, and your service helps form their opinion—good or bad. In a moment of personal reflection, ask yourself if your service to others is making the meal appealing?

Second, if you have eaten the bread of life, your daily decisions play a significant role in whether or not someone is interested in the bread served at the Table. When you put God's principles into action in your life, you create an appealing aroma that draws people to the bread of life. On the other hand, when you claim to eat the bread, then follow your own plans, you create a stench that pushes others away. Take some time to question whether you are creating an aroma that draws others to the bread of life or pushes them away.

LIFT IT UP

God designed an incredible plan for serving the bread of life. When the Table is functioning based on its two-fold purpose of building believers and serving seekers, it is the perfect place to dine. The Table must be balanced in order to avoid the dangers of becoming one sided.

What can you do personally to help ensure that the ultimate food gets the ultimate presentation at the Table?

_____

_____

_____

Prayer Requests:

_____

_____

_____

_____

_____

THE TABLE THE TWO-FOLD PURPOSE

Notes:

_____

_____

_____

_____

_____

_____

_____

_____

_____

_____

_____

_____

_____

_____

_____

_____

_____

STEP IT UP

Take a step further over the next few days and spend some time reflecting on the following devotional thoughts that reinforce the previous session. Use these as reminders to take what you've learned and apply it to your everyday life.

DAY 1

And he is the head of the body, the church; he is the beginning and the firstborn from among the dead, so that in everything he might have the supremacy. -- Colossians 1:18

For the husband is the head of the wife as Christ is the head of the church, his body, of which he is the Savior. -- Ephesians 5:23

In driver's education they teach you many things that you ignore as soon as you get your license. But there are also some things that stick with you. One important lesson is learning how to check your blind spot. The instructors teach you to check your mirrors, then glance over your shoulder to check your blind spot. Inevitably, as a new driver turns his or her head to check the blind spot, they unknowingly steer the car in that same direction. A glance over the right shoulder and the car drifts right. The car, an extension of the body, follows where the head leads.

The church is described as the body of Christ. If Jesus is the head, then the body should follow the direction of Jesus. A body that does not co-operate with the head results in disability. Are you disabling the body by not following Christ's lead? Pray and ask God to show you any area where you are disabling the body by not following the head.

Notes:

_____

_____

_____

_____

_____

_____

_____

_____

_____

_____

Prayer Requests:

_____

_____

_____

_____

_____

_____

_____

_____

_____

DAY 2

They devoted themselves to the apostles' teaching and to the fellowship, to the breaking of bread and to prayer. Everyone was filled with awe, and many wonders and miraculous signs were done by the apostles. All the believers were together and had everything in common. Selling their possessions and goods, they gave to anyone as he had need. Every day they continued to meet together in the temple courts. They broke bread in their homes and ate together with glad and sincere hearts, praising God and enjoying the favor of all the people. And the Lord added to their number daily those who were being saved. -- Acts 2:42-47

The early church was arguably the most dynamic point in church history. In one day God added 3000 to the church. From that point on, these new Christ-followers were the "body" following Jesus' example as the head. While Jesus walked the earth, he was all about building believers and serving seekers. The early church continued this and experienced great favor with God. When these verses are studied, many times the focus is put on how close the believers were to one another. But they were not exclusive in their relationships with each other.

The believers sold their possessions and gave to "anyone" who was in need. These believers loved their time together with other believers, but they were also actively sought out people outside the walls of their church. They served those who were seeking Jesus, and the result was daily addition to the body.

Are you balancing your time building believers with time serving seekers? To contribute to a healthy body, you must do both. Keep asking yourself this question over the coming week as you study the example Jesus set.

Notes:

_____

_____

_____

_____

_____

_____

_____

_____

_____

_____

Prayer Requests:

_____

_____

_____

_____

_____

_____

_____

_____

_____

_____

DAY 3

When they had finished eating, Jesus said to Simon Peter, "Simon son of John, do you truly love me more than these?" "Yes, Lord," he said, "you know that I love you." Jesus said, "Feed my lambs." Again Jesus said, "Simon son of John, do you truly love me?" He answered, "Yes, Lord, you know that I love you." Jesus said, "Take care of my sheep." The third time he said to him, "Simon son of John, do you love me?" Peter was hurt because Jesus asked him the third time, "Do you love me?" He said, "Lord, you know all things; you know that I love you." Jesus said, "Feed my sheep." -- John 21:15-17

The first time parents leave their child with a babysitter can be an interesting event. Generally, the parents will prepare a set of instructions for the two hour separation that looks more like a novel than a checklist. There are times, measurements, and suggestions, as well as rules. The parents will tell the babysitter the same thing several times—just to make sure they get it. The parents want to emphasize what their child needs as they entrust their loved one into the hands of another.

This is similar to the picture in this story in John. Jesus is entrusting his loved ones to those he trained and he wants to make sure they know what to do. The sheep are those who follow Jesus—the church. Jesus was determined for Peter and the disciples to continue feeding them, just as Jesus had fed them.

It is not the only thing that should happen, but a church should definitely be a place where believers are fed. How are believers fed at your church? Spend time in prayer asking God to give you a new perspective on all the ways believers are fed at your church.

THE TABLE

Notes:

_____

_____

_____

_____

_____

_____

_____

_____

_____

Prayer Requests:

_____

_____

_____

_____

_____

_____

_____

_____

_____

DAY 4

Sitting down, Jesus called the Twelve and said, "If anyone wants to be first, he must be the very last, and the servant of all." He took a little child and had him stand among them. Taking him in his arms, he said to them, "Whoever welcomes one of these little children in my name welcomes me; and whoever welcomes me does not welcome me but the one who sent me." -- Mark 9:35-37

Most organizations are built on the principle that the higher up the pyramid of power you are, the more people serve you. Presidents and CEO's have the corner office, the premier parking space, the myriad of assistants, and more. The power players of most companies do not take the time to serve those under them.

Jesus flipped the pyramid of power by teaching his disciples the opposite of the traditional customs of that day. Jesus taught them the sign of a power player in God's kingdom is serving others. And he illustrated his point by taking a child, who in that day was considered very insignificant, and told his disciples to welcome even him. Jesus built the disciples up by breaking down the pyramid of power.

Who do you serve? Jesus taught 360 degree service. This means serving those above you, below you and on your level. Are you following God's design for service or your own design?

Notes:

_____

_____

_____

_____

_____

_____

_____

_____

_____

_____

Prayer Requests:

_____

_____

_____

_____

_____

_____

_____

_____

DAY 5

As Jesus went on from there, he saw a man named Matthew sitting at the tax collector's booth. "Follow me," he told him, and Matthew got up and followed him. While Jesus was having dinner at Matthew's house, many tax collectors and "sinners" came and ate with him and his disciples. When the Pharisees saw this, they asked his disciples, "Why does your teacher eat with tax collectors and 'sinners'?" On hearing this, Jesus said, "It is not the healthy who need a doctor, but the sick. 13But go and learn what this means: 'I desire mercy, not sacrifice.' For I have not come to call the righteous, but sinners." -- Matthew 9:9-13

Think back to when you read about how Jesus built believers and served seekers. Jesus called Matthew to follow him, he called Matthew to serve the seekers around him. So Matthew hosted a dinner to introduce his friends to Jesus. He wanted them to experience the transformation that Jesus offered. Jesus was excited for the opportunity to be around non-believers and share with them. It was the religious people of the day that had a problem with associating with the unreligious people—something Jesus actively sought to do.

Be ready, when you start reaching out and serving seekers; the "religious people" of your day are going to question you, too. There is a balance of keeping yourself pure and being around non-believers, so be careful to keep that balance in check as Jesus did. But, do not separate yourself from those who do not believe because Jesus wants you to serve them like he did.

You have been reading how Jesus taught his disciples to serve others. It continues with serving those outside the church as well. Who are the non-believers you are serving?

THE TABLE

Notes:

_____

_____

_____

_____

_____

_____

_____

_____

_____

Prayer Requests:

_____

_____

_____

_____

_____

_____

_____

_____

_____

THE CHAIRS

START IT UP

Think back to your family's holiday meals or a time when all the family got together. Picture the set up with all the food. Imagine the table and the multitude of chairs surrounding the table for all the guests. In your home, was there an adult table as well a kid's table? Talk about it with the group, as well as what determined the seating arrangement. Which table was the most popular?

TALK IT UP

Just as it was important where you sat at that family meal, the chairs around God's Table are important. In homes, the chairs can represent important positions of honor, such as the head of the table. In the church, the chairs are important as well, but not because of positions of honor. The chairs are a way to make sure the Table is accomplishing its two-fold purpose. If the church is doing what it should, then there should be four chairs around the Table.

THE CHEF

At every meal, someone has to prepare the food. In the church, the pastor or lead communicator represents the dude with food. It is the responsibility of the pastor to prepare a creative and compelling meal for the rest of the Table.

Read 2 Timothy 2:15

The pastor must correctly handle the word of truth. In other words, he must get the recipe right in order to serve the proper food at the Table. This is a big responsibility. Paul knew the weight of this responsibility and that is why he wrote the following:

Read Ephesians 6:19

How often do you think about your pastors and pray for them? How does it make you feel to realize you can play a significant role in the meal by praying for the pastors? What are some of the things you think are important to pray for your pastor?

_____

_____

_____

The pastor is also responsible for preparing a meal that is appetizing and nourishing for all three chairs at the Table. If the church is healthy, the three chairs will be represented by equal thirds.

CHAIR #1

Every Table needs a third of its chairs to be used by mature believers. These are people who are not only eating, but also serving at the Table. So, to be a mature believer there must also be service.

Read Hebrews 5:14

The book of Hebrews teaches mature believers to eat and then to constantly use that source of nutrition for exercise. They stand up from the Table and serve. Many believers get tempted to stay bellied up to the Table and gorge themselves with food. They become diet driven; they are only concerned about eating.

Why do you think it can be so tempting for Christ followers to become diet driven?

_____

_____

_____

    The Bible teaches that a mature believer combines diet with exercise. Christ set this example himself with the following statement:

Read John 4:34

Share some ways you have been fed from serving.

_____

_____

_____

    If the mature are pushing back from the Table and serving others, the second chair will be full.

CHAIR #2

    When the church is building believers and serving seekers, new people will constantly taste the bread of life. The mature will spiritually reproduce leading to baby believers, who are represented by the second chair. And these baby believers also have a responsibility.

Read 1 Peter 2:1-3

    Before feeding on the bread of life, baby believers fed on food that produced ungodly actions. Now having tasted the bread of life, it is time to get rid of that old behavior. This comes from two things. First, you begin to crave pure spiritual milk. Pure spiritual milk is the foundation of the faith such as Christ being the only way to heaven and loving God as well as others.

Think about your life as a new believer. What helped you get pure spiritual milk to grow?

_____

_____

_____

Babies can become diet driven, just like adults. So it is important for them to also exercise. Exercise for babies consists of learning how to use what they have. They learn how to move their arms and coordinate their hands. Their legs become strengthened and they gain balance so they can walk. This happens in baby believers as well by discovering the gifts God has given you to serve.

If you already serve, how did you get plugged into the area where you serve? What advice can you offer those who are trying to find a place to serve?

_____

_____

_____

The baby believers will one day grow to spiritual maturity, but they do not have to wait until maturity to partner with the mature in helping to fill the final chair.

CHAIR #3

Every church should also have a third of its chairs filled with spiritual seekers. These are people who have not yet decided to dine on the bread of life. The lives of the believers give off an appealing aroma for the bread of life, but the seekers have yet to taste it. This aroma is created by believers' actions and decisions. If the actions and decisions are right, it will lead to seekers accepting invitations to come to the Table.

What situations has God placed you in where you can be an appealing aroma?

_____

_____

_____

In your opinion, what are some of the most important decisions a believer can make to give off an appealing aroma to others?

_____

_____

_____

LIFT IT UP

The different chairs at the Table are extremely important, because each of those chairs represents a diverse group of people. Being unbalanced can create church chaos. It is the responsibility of every attendee to fulfill the role of the chair they sit in. But what chair you sit in is not a sign of prestige or power. In fact, the most humble of all the chairs should be those who are the most mature. With this in mind, discuss the following question:

After hearing the responsibilities of each chair, what responsibility do you need to work on to make sure the Table stays healthy?

_____

_____

_____

_____

Prayer Requests:

_____

_____

_____

_____

_____

_____

_____

Notes:

_____

_____

_____

_____

_____

_____

_____

THE TABLE

Notes:

_____

_____

_____

_____

_____

_____

_____

_____

_____

_____

_____

_____

_____

_____

_____

_____

_____

STEP IT UP

Take a step further over the next few days and spend some time reflecting on the following devotional thoughts that reinforce the previous session. Use these as reminders to take what you've learned and apply it to your everyday life.

DAY 1

Do your best to present yourself to God as one approved, a workman who does not need to be ashamed and who correctly handles the word of truth. -- 2 Timothy 2:15

A hospital in Dallas, Texas has an interesting display of hand sculptures. The hands tell a unique story of each individual. There is a molding of an enormous man and his fingers are the size of two or three normal fingers put together. A famous basketball player's fingers are displayed and they are fascinatingly long and athletic. There is another set of a wrestler's fingers which have been broken numerous times and healed in crooked ways. Each set of hands tells an interesting story.

The sum of your decisions tells an interesting story about you, as well. What do your decisions say about you? When you add up the decisions of your life, are you proud of the story they tell? One day God will review the sum of your decisions. As you think about your life's work being on display before God, does it make you proud or ashamed? God wants us to strive for decisions that he will approve, not decisions that we will be ashamed of.

The first decision we need to make to avoid being shamed before God is to choose his Son's offer of forgiveness. Once you have made that decision your life should then be about showing your gratitude through your decisions. What story does the sum of your decisions tell about you?

God wants us to handle his word of truth correctly. We should not carelessly or flippantly read it. We should take time to think about what we are reading and consider what decisions we need to make to align our lives life with the principles and promises we read. This takes consistency and commitment. You must consistently read God's word and apply it to your life. The commitment comes when you get done

reading—it is a commitment to live out what you learned.

Are you correctly handling the word of truth? Pray for God to give you the courage and strength to carry out what you learn on a daily basis.

Notes:

_____

_____

_____

_____

_____

_____

_____

_____

_____

Prayer Requests:

_____

_____

_____

_____

_____

_____

DAY 2

And pray in the Spirit on all occasions with all kinds of prayers and requests. With this in mind, be alert and always keep on praying for all the saints. Pray also for me, that whenever I open my mouth, words may be given me so that I will fearlessly make known the mystery of the gospel. -- Ephesians 6:18-19

The Guinness Book of World Records is filled with incredible feats, both amazing and ridiculous. The following record falls into the latter category. There is a world record for balancing a car on your head. If you do not believe it, go to the web page and look it up. You can even check out the picture. The record for balancing a car on a human head is around 30 seconds. The weight of carrying a car on your head for 30 seconds is something most of us could never imagine.

Along those same lines, the pastor carries a huge weight of responsibility while leading the church. It is a tremendous weight that far exceeds 30 seconds of holding up a car. Paul knew this weight and that is exactly why he asked for others to pray for him to be faithful in his carrying out his duty. If Paul needed prayer, your pastor today needs prayer as well. By praying for him, you are partnering with him and with God to make your church everything God desires.

Brainstorm a list of things to pray for your pastor and start today.

Notes:

_____

_____

_____

_____

_____

_____

_____

_____

_____

Prayer Requests:

_____

_____

_____

_____

_____

_____

_____

_____

DAY 3

But solid food is for the mature, who by constant use have trained themselves to distinguish good from evil. -- Hebrews 5:14

The author of Hebrews is writing to Christ followers and instructing them how to live. He wants to instruct them in more complicated things as well, but they are not ready. He likens this principle to feeding a baby solid food. Just like a baby needs the simple nourishment of milk, the immature in their faith need simple principles they can digest.

Mature believers can handle more complicated principles. The problem is that most of us assume we are mature. This is like asking a high school student if they are a good driver. Almost every student is going to answer with a resounding, "Of course I am!" But the reality is most of them are not. Can you honestly evaluate your spiritual maturity?

Spiritual maturity is marked by constantly living out the fundamental principles of faith. Do you love God with everything inside of you? Do you love those around you the way Jesus loved those around him? Do you hate and avoid evil? Do you share your faith with those around you as opportunities arise? Do you do all of this constantly?

Pray for God to give you an honest evaluation of your spiritual maturity and show you where you need to grow.

THE TABLE THE CHAIRS

Notes:

_____

_____

_____

_____

_____

_____

_____

_____

_____

_____

Prayer Requests:

_____

_____

_____

_____

_____

_____

_____

_____

_____

DAY 4

We who are strong ought to bear with the failings of the weak and not to please ourselves. Each of us should please his neighbor for his good, to build him up. -- Romans 15:1-2

Reality T.V. shows are still very popular. You get to watch a group of people interact in an unusual setting as they compete for the ultimate prize. There are strategies, alliances and lots of lies. One moment a contestant is helping out another contestant, and the next day that same contestant will stab them in the back. The motives are impure, so the assistance offered is rarely helpful.

What are your motives when you help someone else? If you help others for what you get out of it, your help can be less than helpful. New believers need help, and as a member of the church you have a responsibility to help them. But helping them does not just consist of doing what it takes to ease your conscience. Helping them is about moving beyond you and focusing on their needs.

Jesus moved beyond what he wanted and helped those in need. Spend a minute checking your motives. When you serve others is it for you or for them? Pray and ask God to help you develop the right motives in serving.

Notes:

_____

_____

_____

_____

_____

_____

_____

_____

_____

_____

Prayer Requests:

_____

_____

_____

_____

_____

_____

_____

_____

_____

_____

DAY 5

"My food," said Jesus, "is to do the will of him who sent me and to finish his work." -- John 4:34

You've learned that spiritual maturity comes from putting the principles God teaches into practice. Jesus went as far as to say doing the will of God is what actually fed him. Jesus knew that as you obey the principles of God, you will grow in your relationship with him, maturing into a strong believer.

Every time you take a chance and share your faith with someone, you learn something about God's desire for everyone to know him. The act of humbling yourself to put someone else's time above yours in helping them with a problem teaches you about the servant nature of Jesus. Resisting the temptation to sin connects you with Jesus in his temptations while on earth. And following the will of God feeds your relationship with him.

How have you grown spiritually from doing the will of God?

THE TABLE THE CHAIRS

Notes:

_____

_____

_____

_____

_____

_____

_____

_____

_____

Prayer Requests:

_____

_____

_____

_____

_____

_____

_____

_____

_____

THE TABLE

PUTTING THE PIECES TOGETHER

START IT UP

For five weeks we have looked at the different pieces of the Table. The examination started with the cosmic carbohydrate. The bread of life is served and provides satisfaction like no other meal. This ultimate meal is served at the Table where the ultimate presentation is the goal. We learned that the Table serves the bread of life, so its presentation must be done with excellence. Finally, the chairs were discussed and everyone found their place. The pieces of this meal are incredible, but just studying the separate pieces does not do it justice.

Just looking at the pieces without seeing the big picture is like walking in to a movie for 15 minutes one day, then coming back for another 15 minutes the next day and keeping this pattern up until you have seen the entire movie. You will see some great scenes, but you will miss the magnificence of the movie.

What is your favorite scene from a movie you really enjoy? Describe the scene and tell why you like it.

TALK IT UP

There are many incredible scenes in movies, but the scene isolated from the rest of the movie is not the same. The piece lacks power and brilliance without the rest of the story. The pieces of the Table might seem lacking in power and brilliance without seeing how they all fit together. Take what you have discussed over the past weeks, and relive those pieces in the context of the big picture. This will give you the opportunity to see one of the greatest scenes of all time.

THE INVITATION

The scene starts in offices throughout the city, in homes, in neighborhoods, in health clubs, and in restaurants. Members of the family who have tasted the bread of life interact with dozens of people on a daily basis. This interaction has the opportunity for a distinct aroma.

Read 1 Peter 2:9-12

What are some of the phrases used to describe Christ followers in these verses? Explain what you think they mean.

_____

_____

_____

As Christ followers, what actions are we called to take?

_____

_____

What can the response of non-believers be when we follow Christ?

_____

_____

A Christ follower, a.k.a. a family member who is fleshing out what they fed on, provides a distinct aroma. This aroma is appealing to non-believers and sparks curiosity and a craving to taste what the Christ follower has tasted. Members of the family, who stand up from the Table and are exercising, take advantage of others' cravings and extend invitations to the Table.

THE PREPARATION

While the family members are in the community inviting those around them to the Table, the chefs are preparing a creative and compelling meal. The chefs are the pastors, and they work diligently to prepare a meal appropriate for the occasion. The chefs are trying to balance the two-fold purpose of building believers and serving seekers as they prepare the meal.

What have been some of the most creative and compelling elements you have seen at church? How have those you invited to the Table responded to the elements?

_____

_____

_____

_____

The recipes are tested and tried until they are just right. The balance is considered and the adjustments are made. The plans are brought to fruition on a weekly basis for the weekend services. With the invitations of the family members and the preparations of the chefs in place, it is time for the presentation of the ultimate meal.

THE PRESENTATION

It is the weekend and time for the family, as well as the guests, to gather around the Table and enjoy the meal. People cannot be made to eat the bread of life, so all that is left to do is to present it in the most creative and compelling way possible. The presentation must be just right, in hopes that the appealing aroma of the family, the creative communication of the chefs, and the Holy Spirit can bring those around the Table to a point where they taste the bread of life.

When you were younger, what did your family do when it was time to entertain guests? How many of those traditions do you still apply at your home today?

_____

_____

_____

There is an incredible amount of work involved before the food is served. Some of it you are aware of; other things go on behind the scenes. There are thousands of family members every weekend working to make sure nothing distracts from the meal.

Try to brainstorm all the volunteer positions happening on a weekend in your church and discuss how each position contributes to the presentation.

_____

_____

_____

The food is served as the music plays and the message engages the audience. Everyone gets the opportunity to dine together on the bread of life. Some taste it for the very first time. Hungers that have ached for years are finally satisfied. Tangible needs are met by the principles of the Bible, as well as spiritual needs that had no other hope of satisfaction. It is an incredible event.

LIFT IT UP

The meal concludes as the family stands up from the Table and goes out to exercise fulfilling the requirements for a healthy believer. As they exercise, the invitation begins again, along with the preparation by the chefs for next week's meal. What an incredible scene directed by our great God!

THE TABLE

Read Ephesians 4:11-13

How does it make you feel to read about God's incredible plan and to realize that you are a part of this incredible event he has been planning and serving for 2000 years?

_____

_____

_____

God's plan is incredible! It is an honor to be a part of what he is doing. Finish tonight by dedicating your time of prayer to the Table. Pray for family and guests who will attend. Pray for those preparing the meal, as well as those serving the meal. Pray for your opportunity to be an appealing aroma as well as those around you drawn by the appealing aroma to the Table.

Prayer Requests:

_____

_____

_____

_____

_____

_____

_____

_____

STEP IT UP

Take a step further over the next few days and spend some time reflecting on the following devotional thoughts that reinforce the previous session. Use these as reminders to take what you've learned and apply it to your everyday life.

DAY 1

Dear friends, I urge you, as aliens and strangers in the world, to abstain from sinful desires, which war against your soul. Live such good lives among the pagans that, though they accuse you of doing wrong, they may see your good deeds and glorify God on the day he visits us. -- 1 Peter 2:11-12

Most people have an aroma that brings back memories. Is there an aroma that does that for you? Maybe it is a family member's cooking, or your favorite restaurant that can instantly move you from full to hungry. Aromas can be powerful things.

God wants us to be an appealing aroma for him. Our actions should create an appealing aroma so that even those who are not interested in God will become hungry for him. This comes from abstaining from sinful desires. You must set aside your desire to be prideful because it stinks. Your greed and lust give off a serious sewage stink. Self-centeredness and hypocrisy will not make anyone hungry for God. Give up those selfish desires and get with God's good life.

Spiritually speaking, how do you smell to those around you?

Notes:

_____

_____

_____

_____

_____

_____

_____

_____

_____

_____

Prayer Requests:

_____

_____

_____

_____

_____

_____

_____

_____

_____

_____

DAY 2

My prayer is not that you take them out of the world but that you protect them from the evil one. They are not of the world, even as I am not of it. Sanctify them by the truth; your word is truth. As you sent me into the world, I have sent them into the world. -- John 17:15-18

Do you know any Christ followers who have completely separated from anything non-Christian? They only eat at Christian owned restaurants and wear clothes with Christian logos. Their bumpers are a collection of catchy slogans and one sentence messages letting everyone know they are different. If you ask them about a television show or movie that is not produced by a Christian owned organization, they will have no idea what you are talking about.

People who line up with this kind of thinking are missing the point of Jesus' prayer in John 17. The phrase commonly used to describe what you read in John is "In the world but not of the world." Jesus knew those who believe in him would be different, simply by applying his principles. This difference would protect them as well as cause them to be a light. With this in mind, Jesus sent his believers back into the world.

How separated from non-believers are you? God never called you to live on another planet when you accepted his Son. If God wanted you that separated, he would have taken you to heaven the moment you accepted Jesus. God's plan is for you to live a God-guided life in the middle of everyone else. Reread the verses for today and evaluate your separation from those who do not believe in Jesus.

THE TABLE

Notes:

_____

_____

_____

_____

_____

_____

_____

_____

_____

Prayer Requests:

_____

_____

_____

_____

_____

_____

_____

_____

DAY 3

"My prayer is not for them alone. I pray also for those who will believe in me through their message, that all of them may be one, Father, just as you are in me and I am in you. May they also be in us so that the world may believe that you have sent me." -- John 17:20-21

Have you ever had someone pray over you? It can be a very powerful experience as you have someone go to God on your behalf and ask for things you need. The experience is heightened when it is by someone you know is in intimate fellowship with God. It seems like those people know exactly what to say to God on your behalf.

What you read today is Jesus praying over you. That is a snippet of his prayer for all the believers to come. Read the prayer again now that you realize it is for you.

Now that you have read it again, think about this. Of all the things Jesus could ask on your behalf, he asked for unity with other believers. Jesus knew there is power when believers unite. They can accomplish incredible things.

Are you united with other believers the way Jesus desired? If you are unsure, the next few days will help clear it up. If you are united, the next couple days will cement your purpose in unity.

THE TABLE **PUTTING THE PIECES TOGETHER**

Notes:

_____

_____

_____

_____

_____

_____

_____

_____

_____

_____

Prayer Requests:

_____

_____

_____

_____

_____

_____

_____

_____

_____

DAY 4

It was he who gave some to be apostles, some to be prophets, some to be evangelists, and some to be pastors and teachers, to prepare God's people for works of service, so that the body of Christ may be built up until we all reach unity in the faith and in the knowledge of the Son of God and become mature, attaining to the whole measure of the fullness of Christ. -- Ephesians 4:11-13

You are an important part of the team. When it comes to being a Christ follower, no one is allowed to sit the bench, because everyone is needed. God gave every believer a talent or ability to be used in building up the body. When the individual parts of the body are working together, the entire body will become strong and able to accomplish the goal of looking like Christ.

What part of the body are you? God has given you the ability to contribute to the overall health of the body, so you do have a place. Are you energetic and outgoing? Maybe your place is greeting in the church. If you are more of the rugged outdoor type, the parking ministry might be a fit. Do you have a compassionate heart and a desire to lead? A small group leader could be your place. Where do you fit?

Spend a couple minutes thinking about your personality as well as likes and dislikes. Then, think of opportunities to serve in the church and where you might fit.

Notes:

_____

_____

_____

_____

_____

_____

_____

_____

_____

_____

Prayer Requests:

_____

_____

_____

_____

_____

_____

_____

_____

_____

DAY 5

From him the whole body, joined and held together by every supporting ligament, grows and builds itself up in love, as each part does its work. -- Ephesians 4:16

Do you remember group projects in junior high and high school? It always seemed like there was one person who did 90% of the work. If that one person was you, it is probably still a bitter memory. For those of you who rode the coattails of the brain in your group it was a pretty sweet ride. All you had to do was sign your name on the project and you got the same grade as everyone else, even if you did no work.

Group projects do not work that way in the church. Everyone has a role to fill and a responsibility to the body. The body is most successful when "each part does its work." That means if you not doing your part, you cannot just rely on someone else. You have a unique role to fill that no other person can. When you try to just slide in at the end of the project and sign your name, you hurt the entire body.

Are you playing your part in the body? Or are you relying on others to carry you? Playing your part means bringing your tithe to the church, volunteering in ministries at the church, inviting your friends and supporting the direction of the church. You were designed for this, so do not miss the opportunity.

Notes:

_____

_____

_____

_____

_____

_____

_____

_____

_____

Prayer Requests:

_____

_____

_____

_____

_____

_____

_____

_____

_____

INTRODUCTION

CREATIVE NOTES

ICEBREAKERS

Idea – Six Course Meal

SNACK – For the duration of the study, serve six different "courses" for the snack time.

- Week 1 – Appetizers
- Week 2 – Soups
- Week 3 – Salads
- Week 4 – Entrees
- Week 5 – Desserts
- Week 6 – Fruit and Cheese Trays

Idea – Q&A

DISCUSSION – Ask a question that will engage the group and provide a natural lead-in to the rest of your discussion. Those questions might be something like:

- What is your favorite restaurant for ambiance?
- If you could dine with anyone, who would it be and why?
- Name a restaurant you go to because they make a dish better than any other place.
- Name something that has ruined a dining experience for you.
- What are some things that would be on your list for a good dining experience?

BRIDGE – This series explores the topic of the Table by examining the ultimate dining experience as designed by God. God desires to feed everyone with his dining design and you play a crucial role.

HANDS-ON ACTIVITIES

Activity – "Waiter, there's a fly in my soup."

GUIDELINES/INSTRUCTIONS – Have several group members role play a nice dining experience and bad dining experience.

BRIDGE – God considered your needs as well as the obstacles of real life and came up with a solution. His food brings satisfaction like no other. His environment is carefully crafted to provide just the right elements to entice and engage every audience. The guest list is diverse and interesting, bringing a mix of people from all social situations. Best yet, you are invited to this dining experience and you can bring a guest, or two, or as many as you can bring with you.

Activity – "I can't, I have to wash my hair that night..."

GUIDELINES/INSTRUCTIONS – Break into small groups. Give each group a set of magazines and have them make a poster of obstacles that get in the way of people going to church.

BRIDGE – God knew there would be obstacles in getting the ultimate meal to everyone. Because of this, he designed the ultimate environment to serve the bread of life to those hungering for a satisfaction that will not fade.

Activity – "Let them eat cake..."

GUIDELINES/INSTRUCTIONS – Have a cake on a table in the middle of the group. Ask, "Can the table give you cake? How can we get a piece of the cake?" (Note: Do this during the environment lesson)

BRIDGE – At the Table, the pastor is the dude with the food. He serves up the bread of life, but all those at the Table are not supposed to just eat and remain still. It is the job of the family to not only eat, but also to help serve the guests at the Table.

Activity – Bake Bread

GUIDELINES/INSTRUCTIONS – Have bread dough ready when members arrive. Let each person make their own design or shape. The bread can be baked during the lesson then enjoyed as a snack afterwards, or given as a "take home."

BRIDGE – God knew when the word got out about the ultimate food, there would be millions wanting to taste the cosmic carbohydrate. He has tailor made the word to reach each and every life, just as we have specifically designed our personal bread.

THE TABLE INTRODUCTION

VISUAL REINFORCEMENTS

- Have copies of menus and nutritional information from restaurant websites.
- Have building blocks and serving utensils to represent building believers and serving seekers.
- Try a food theme for a formal dinner and let everyone sit around a big table for the lesson.
- Set a table with crystal, china and candles – leaders set the table.
- Bring a bottle of "Superfood™" (made by Odwalla®) to represent the cosmic carbohydrate.
- Print off copies of different volunteer positions at your church. Encourage members to volunteer.
- Have Volunteer Applications available at your small group meeting as well as information on any classes your church has to help people discover their spiritual gifts and where they can best serve.

POSSIBLE MEDIA REINFORCEMENTS

- Play a scene of Bob eating dinner in the movie "What About Bob?" (Chapter 9 in the movie at 49:30)

TAKE HOME OBJECT (Reminders of the lesson)

- Volunteer Applications
- Serving utensils (can get inexpensive ones from a dollar store)
- Bake miniature loaves of bread for everyone with a "Bread of Life" ribbon or wrapper

MISCELLANEOUS

- Send out invitations to the "Dinner Party"
- Send a small group meeting reminder designed as a menu

LEADER'S NOTES

How has God satisfied a specific need in your life?

God meets the needs of both believers and non-believers. On a very general basis, God provides the sun and rain that feed the plants. Homes, cars and other possessions are ultimately provided by God. So, the question about God providing is not about "if" it is much more about being aware of "how" God provides.

If individuals are struggling with thinking of how God has met a need, help them by encouraging them to think about their basic needs. Once they have identified basic needs, help them consider how each need is satisfied. Show them how God has acted in their lives to provide for them, maybe without their even realizing it.

Why do you think Jesus described himself as the bread of life?

The "bread of life" term comes from an ongoing conversation Jesus is having with this particular group of followers. Shortly before his description, Jesus fed a crowd of 5000 with five loaves of bread and two fish. This crowd followed Jesus, so he took the opportunity to teach them.

In John 6:25-29, Jesus told the crowd they were only looking for more food. Jesus then encouraged them to work for eternal food. In doing this, Jesus began to reveal his role as the Messiah which greatly interested the crowd. Jesus let them know he was sent from God.

In verses 30-33, the conversation changes so Jesus could prove he was from God. The crowd brings up how God provided manna in the desert for those following Moses. The crowd even quotes Nehemiah 9:15, describing the manna as "bread from heaven." Jesus explained to them it was not Moses who provided the bread, but God. And, Jesus explained, God wanted to provide them with true bread.

When the crowd asked for the true bread, Jesus said, "I am the bread of life." This comment carries several implications. First, it is part of several "I AM" statements Jesus made showing his divinity by using the name God used to introduce himself to Moses. Second, Jesus uses bread to describe how he had been provided by God to meet their needs. Finally, Jesus is showing them that if they come to him, he will satisfy their desires on an ongoing basis.

How has the bread of life satisfied hungers in your life that were not satisfied before?

Jesus has a way of satisfying hungers that seemed impossible to satisfy. The apostle Paul knew this and described it in Philippians 4:11, "… I have learned to be content whatever the circumstances." With Jesus, the insatiable greed for money can be fulfilled righteously by Jesus for the first time. Physical lusts can be transformed and satisfied like never before. The list goes on and on, but the important part is that all is possible through a relationship with God.

What do you think are some obstacles standing in the way of more people tasting the bread of life?

There are many answers, but there are a few that will be the most common in your discussion. Priorities are a huge obstacle. It is not that some lack the desire to taste the bread of life, but when it comes to actually eating the bread, there are too many things higher on the ladder of priorities.

Previous experiences with "church" people can also be a common obstacle. Unfortunately, some of the loudest individuals identified with the church are commonly the worst representatives. Oftentimes their beliefs are unusual, and their lifestyles make it difficult to be around them.

Finally, there is the duo of doubt and/or fear. When you stop to think about the belief in a man who claimed to be God, who died on the cross, but lives today, it is difficult to swallow. It is scary to think about giving the steering wheel of your life to somebody who can be so difficult to believe in.

There will be many different answers. Do not feel like you have to solve the obstacles mentioned. Some of the obstacles have been present for years, and they will only be overcome by the work of the Holy Spirit.

What are ways the family serves at the Table on a weekly basis?

Serving at the Table is not reserved for public positions only. The pastors and the worship leaders definitely serve at the Table, but it takes many more each week. Servants at the Table provide help that ranges from those serving groups of babies, children, students and adults, to those behind the scenes twisting knobs and turning dials. All of the volunteer positions contribute to serving at the Table because they all help the bread of life get to those who need it.

Remember the two-fold purpose of the Table: to build believers and to serve seekers. Based on the purpose of the Table, describe what the guest list of the table should look like.

If the purpose is two-fold, the guest list should be two-fold as well. There should be a group who believe in Christ and what the Bible teaches. These individuals range from brand new believers to those who have believed for a long time. There should also be a group who do not believe. The church is a great place to explore the truth. If a non-believer cannot come to the church to get truth, where are they going to get truth? If the church is following Jesus' model, it should have both believers and non-believers.

How do the thirds being present at the Table prove that the church is fulfilling the two-fold purpose of building believers and serving seekers?

If the groups are doing what they should be doing, all three groups will naturally develop. If all the believers are inviting seekers, there will be a healthy amount of seekers coming to explore the truth in your church. If the seekers are being taught the truth, they will eventually cross the line of Christianity and become new believers. As they grow in their faith, they will ultimately transition from the baby stage of belief into a stage of maturity. When all these are happening in a healthy balance, the thirds will develop.

WHAT'S COOKING? - PART 1

CREATIVE NOTES

ICEBREAKERS

Idea – Q&A

DISCUSSION – Ask a question or two that will engage the group and provide a natural lead-in to the rest of your discussion. Those questions might be something like:

- What is a food that you loved to eat, ate too much and then got tired of eating?
- Name a situation that has helped you grow where God provided for a need of yours.
- What are some things you currently complain about that you could turn around as an opportunity to thank God instead?

BRIDGE – God provided a long term, creative cuisine for His people twice in history. The first example happened almost 1500 years before Jesus walked the earth. God had just freed his people after 400 years of living in another land while being slaves. God worked his Egyptian Escape through one of the most famous figures in Old Testament history – Moses.

HANDS-ON ACTIVITIES

Activity – Comic Strip

GUIDELINES/INSTRUCTIONS – Draw comic strip of Moses and the different parts of his story.

BRIDGE – The people saw God do something incredible for them as Moses began leading them on their journey to the Promised Land. But the gratefulness of the people did not last long. In a short time they were complaining about the same God that just answered their prayers and freed them.

THE TABLE

Activity – "Look What I Made!"

GUIDELINES/INSTRUCTIONS – Once everyone has named a favorite food, provide Play-Doh® for each person and have them mold their favorite food.

BRIDGE – God is a generous provider. He allows us to have all of our favorite foods and more. But, we need to remember to choose his plan, not our own plans as a way of thanking him for his provision.

Activity – Art Project

GUIDELINES/INSTRUCTIONS – Have each person look for multiple pictures of their favorite food and make a collage of them all.

BRIDGE – God is a generous provider. He allows us to have all of our favorite foods and more. But, we need to remember to chose his plan, not own plans as a way of thanking him for his provision.

VISUAL REINFORCEMENTS

- Have a bland food out for everyone (plain grits, plain noodles, dry bread, plain potatoes, plain white rice, etc). Let everyone taste this food, and help them see that they could survive on it even though they would not be totally full or satisfied.
- Have everyone bring a favorite food for snack.

POSSIBLE MEDIA REINFORCEMENTS

- Watch the introduction or conclusion of the documentary "Supersize Me." Note that when you eat all the wrong food, it has negative consequences for the body God gave you.
- Pick your favorite meal – video journal (or write a journal) for one week of eating only this one dish for every meal (breakfast, lunch, and dinner). How did you feel at the beginning of the week? How did you feel by day three? How did you feel on the last day?

TAKE HOME OBJECT (Reminders of the lesson)

- Eat your snack at the end of the meeting instead of at the beginning.
- Make a take home box of "French fries." Make the French fries out of cardstock with different scriptures printed on them.

LEADER'S NOTES

For those who know the story, describe in your own words what God did through Moses to free his people.

For the complete story, you can read Exodus 1-14. The abbreviated story includes how God placed Moses in the house of the Pharaoh from an early age. Moses disobeyed God by murdering an Egyptian guard, so he fled to the desert for 40 years. During that time, God shaped Moses and prepared him to lead the people of God. Moses returned to Egypt, empowered by God and confronted the Pharaoh. God used ten different plagues (water to blood, frogs, gnats, flies, livestock illness, boils, hail, locusts, darkness, the death of every firstborn son) to get the Pharaoh to free Israel from slavery.

After the Pharaoh agreed to let the people of Israel go, he chased them with his army. God parted the Red Sea to allow the Israelites to cross on dry land. When the Egyptians followed the Israelites, the sea closed in on them, destroying the army and ultimately freeing the Israelite people.

How has a hunger in your life caused you to complain and forget how God has provided for you?

It is amazing how easy it is to forget what God has done to bless you. The hungers range from person to person, but they can infect anyone. A hunger for a spouse can cause you to complain about how difficult your life is despite a great job, close friends, and security. A difficult job can cause you to forget about how great your family life is, your good health, and even your success in other areas.

Hunger has a way of distorting views and bringing up the negative. When hunger is attacking you, tell God about it. God is the ultimate satisfier of hunger. When you try to satisfy that hunger on your own, you commonly fall into the temptation to sin.

How has God provided for you even when you asked with the wrong attitude, or even with wrong motives?

It would be great if every time you asked God for something, your attitude was like that of Jesus in the garden, "Yet not as I will, but as you will." In reality, not every thing you ask God for is exclusively for his glory. The incredible thing is that God is so gracious, he sometimes provides for you even when your motive or attitude is not right. In fact, God can use that provision to help you realize the wrong attitudes or motives.

What things does God use to remind you on a regular basis of his power and provision?

God wants you to remember him. He gives you reminders all of the time—from the beauty of his creation to specific comments from friends. God can even get more specific in reminding you. In Deuteronomy 6:8-9, God gave his people these directions about his commands. "Tie them as symbols on your hands and bind them on your foreheads. Write them on the doorframes of your houses and on your gates."

We can follow this encouragement by memorizing Bible verses or writing Bible verses on pieces of paper and placing them in common places. A powerful verse on your bathroom mirror can serve as a great daily reminder.

How has God given you a great gift, but you did not follow his plan with the gift?

The Israelites were given specific instructions accompanying their incredible gift of manna. The Israelites were to take just what they needed for the day, and not try to hoard the provisions from God. This principle is later articulated by Jesus teaching to not worry about tomorrow in Matthew 6:34. It is easy to criticize the Israelites for collecting more than a day's worth, but are you able to apply the principle of not worrying about tomorrow in your own life?

God has given you the great gift of salvation, yet none of us fully obey the instructions that come with this gift. Maybe God gave you a great opportunity at work that you have ignored to this point. Possibly there is a relationship that is a blessing from God that you have not thanked him for. Whatever the example, chances are you can relate to not completely following God's plan with a gift.

In your experience, what happens to God's provision when you use it apart from his plan?

These are experiences, so there is not necessarily a right or wrong answer. Sometimes, misusing a gift can temporarily result in benefit. Other times, the consequences are immediate. One point you might bring up is that God examines the faithfulness of his followers. If they are not faithful with a little, it can cause them to forfeit future blessings (Matthew 25:14-30).

What provisions seem to be the easiest to understand and apply the "manna mentality?"

The answers can be many, but some common answers to expect are money, relationships, success, etc...

What has helped you overcome the manna mentality?

Share from your personal experience. The Bible teaches in 1 Corinthians 10:13, "No temptation has seized you except what is common to man. And God is faithful; he will not let you be tempted beyond what you can bear. But when you are tempted, he will also provide a way out so that you can stand up under it." By sharing experiences you can encourage others and provide answers that were previous undiscovered.

WHAT'S COOKING? - PART 2

CREATIVE NOTES

ICEBREAKERS

Idea – Questions

DISCUSSION – Ask a question or two that will engage the group and provide a natural lead-in to the rest of your discussion. Those questions might be something like:

- What causes people to fail at diets?
- What is a need of yours that God has met?
- What was your favorite Happy Meal™ toy?
- Name something you eat or drink that really doesn't satisfy your hunger or thirst.

BRIDGE – There are a lot of diets out there, and many of them are just fad diets. They may work for a while, but the results cannot be sustained. God, though, designed the definitive diet that has been proven effective for 2000 years. God was preparing this definitive diet when his people got hungry again. He gave them temporary satisfaction with a Hebrew Happy Meal.

HANDS-ON ACTIVITIES

Activity – Bread of Life

GUIDELINES/INSTRUCTIONS – Have several loaves of baked bread on a table and have people take a chunk of bread that represents how much "bread of life" they have in their life.

BRIDGE – Jesus promises fulfillment from eating the bread of life. Some of you have tasted the bread of life, yet you are still unsatisfied. You might be wondering why you are not experiencing the satisfaction you read about. The bread of life is not a snack. God serves only one food for satisfaction, so if you fill your stomach with anything else, you will not find true satisfaction. Satan wants you to cheat on your divine diet.

Others of you are not satisfied because you are just nibbling on the bread of life. God wants you to take big bites. God wants you to taste and see how good life with him can be.

Activity – My Story

GUIDELINES/INSTRUCTIONS – Draw your salvation story (can be collage, comic strip, etc.)

BRIDGE – Jesus describes himself as the "Son of Man" and says that he can offer them a food that endures through eternal life. Jesus knows we have personal needs that need to be satisfied today, but he also knew we would never be satisfied until our spiritual hunger is satisfied. Only Jesus can satisfy the ultimate hunger of our spirit.

Activity – He Has Provided

GUIDELINES/INSTRUCTIONS – Everyone decorate or make a "Happy Meal™" box to show God provisions. It can have games, word finds, etc. It can also use magazine pictures to decorate.

BRIDGE – Jesus provided the people a miraculous Hebrew Happy Meal. But he didn't stop his perplexing provision years ago. He still provides for his people today.

VISUAL REINFORCEMENTS

- Serve a very small snack at the beginning of the meeting (like airline peanuts). Ask the group if the snack satisfied their hunger. Then have hearty bread available for heavier snacking.
- Have some diet books displayed around the room.
- Display the Minimum Daily Nutritional Levels and labels to various food items.
- A print out of nutritional info from McDonald's® or other restaurant (can get this info online).
- Super-sized cups.

POSSIBLE MEDIA REINFORCEMENTS

- Clip from any exercise video.
- Clips of Food Network TV shows that highlight healthy eating, such as "Low Carb and Lovin' It" and "Calorie Commando".

TAKE HOME OBJECT (Reminders of the lesson)

- Happy Meal™ Toys for Hebrew Happy Meal.
- Packs of "Cheese-its®" reminding that God is no snack.

LEADER NOTES

How has Jesus provided for you in an unexpected way?

Ephesians 3:20 describes God as, "Him who is able to do immeasurably more than all we ask or imagine, according to his power that at work within us." When dealing with God, we should expect the unexpected. To gain sons and daughters, he sacrificed his Son. To show his love, he let his creation turn against him.

God meets the needs of his followers today. His methods are often still unexpected. God has a way of providing money in an abnormal way. God can create friendships out of the most unlikely relationships. He can use tragedy to teach and ultimately benefit his followers. God is an expert in the unexpected.

What was your response to his perplexing provision?

Coincidence? I think not! When God provides for you, do not chalk it up to coincidence. There is the old illustration of a man putting a roof on his house. As he was nailing the final pieces to the steep roof, he lost his footing and began to slip. He prayed on his way down, "Lord, please stop me from falling!" About that time, his shirt got hung on a nail and stopped his descent. The roofer's response to God was, "Never mind... the nail caught me."

The God who could send an angel down to catch that man is the same God that can carefully place a random nail. Thank him for both of these divine acts.

How have you seen somebody's perspective about God changed because they had a personal need met?

The Bible is full of personal needs being met. The lame walk, the blind see, the deaf hear, and more. God did not stop meeting specific needs when biblical times ended. God still meets specific needs in individual lives, and it is a powerful testimony about him. God uses his followers today. The figurative shoulder to cry on can become a tangible provision when you allow God to use you.

Allowing God to use you in a specific way in the life of someone around you shows how God knows all of his creation personally. God is no longer some impersonal force to that person. God becomes somebody who is alive and active in his or her life.

How have you seen personal needs drive an individual's life?

We all have specific needs. It does not make you unholy to admit you have a need. God created everyone in need of a personal connection to him. Once that need is met, there are still many more. In Paul's famous passage about contentment (Philippians 4:11-13), he admitted he had times of need. Contentment does not mean ignoring needs. When you find contentment, you trust God to provide for your needs and withstand the times you are in need, based on God's strength.

Since everyone has needs, it is not a sin to want a need fulfilled. It is a sin, however, when you try to satisfy a need apart from God's will. For example, trying to satisfy a sexual need outside of marriage is sin. Seeking the need for personal achievement at the sacrifice of church, family, and more is a sin. Attempting to seek self-worth outside of God is called sin. It can happen to anyone when they try to get their need fixed away from God.

What snacks does Satan try to tempt you with the most?

Be prepared for a myriad of answers. Help those who answer realize temptation and sin are not the same thing. Satan tempted Jesus in the desert (Luke 4), but Jesus was still without sin. Satan wants you to feel defeated when you feel tempted. Do not buy that lie! Victory is in overcoming temptation just as much as avoiding the temptation. That does not mean you should seek temptations to overcome. Satan will send enough to you without you having to look for them. Understand the difference between temptation and the act of carrying through temptation to sin.

How has God helped you overcome your cravings to snack?

Personal illustrations can help a lot in this instance. It is great to say reading your Bible helped, but you might be able to help someone even more by telling a particular verse that helped you. If it is appropriate, share words of encouragement you have been given. By getting specific on this question, you can help those in your group.

What can you do to make sure you are getting plenty of the bread of life?

Some are still craving the cosmic carbohydrate because they are not taking a big enough bite. Being involved in the worship service on a weekly basis is the starting point. Bring something to take notes with during the service, and write down as much as you can. Then, review your notes the next day and pray through what changes you need to make to align your life with what you learned.

Once you are feeding at the main service, add in daily time reading God's Word. Set up a plan to read the Bible for fifteen minutes a day, Monday through Friday. Write down what you learn and what action you need to take based on what you read. Use the devotionals at the end of each session of the study guide as a starting point.

One problem many believers face is that while they are feeding in one or more services a week as well as reading the Bible on their own, they still feel malnourished. The problem could be while they are taking big bites and chewing on it, they are not swallowing what they are chewing on. At some point, what you learn must become what you live. Do not just chew, then spit it out; chew, then live it out.

THE TWO-FOLD PURPOSE

CREATIVE NOTES

ICEBREAKERS:

Idea – Label the Pieces

ACTIVITY – The pieces of a formal place setting each have a purpose. Do you know their purpose? Pair up with someone and label the pieces of a formal place setting diagram (these need to be drawn and/or copied ahead of time). The fastest pair to finish labeling the formal place setting with the most accuracy wins.

BRIDGE – Formal place settings at a table have a purpose. For some of you, it was easy to label the pieces because you are experienced with that setting. Others felt like you were in some Twilight Zone episode. Whether or not you can label a formal place setting does not make you a good person. Your knowledge of the place settings is based on your past experiences.

Idea – Talent Show

DISCUSSION – Have everyone tell their most unique talent and, if possible, demonstrate that talent for the group.

BRIDGE – Every person is created with unique abilities. Those unique abilities are significant in the church. When everyone puts those unique abilities to use in the church, the church becomes more appealing to those who are new.

Idea – Ample Appetizers

ILLUSTRATION – Have several types of breads set out as appetizers when the guests arrive. Let them sample as many of the different breads as they want.

BRIDGE – Jesus is the Bread of Life. The appetizers you set out serve as a reminder that there are many things that people are looking for, but there is only one bread that completely satisfies.

HANDS-ON ACTIVITIES

Activity – Build Them Up

GUIDELINES/INSTRUCTIONS – Break into teams of three to four, giving each a deck of playing cards. Let each team compete against each other for a few minutes trying to build the tallest house of cards.

BRIDGE – This will demonstrate the need to be purposeful in where you place each piece and how it takes balance to be successful.

Activity – Customer Comments

GUIDELINES/INSTRUCTIONS – Prepare "Rate the Service – Comment Cards" Have questions like: "How would you rate yourself on serving at _____."
List different areas that help encourage fellow Christ followers such as: Teaching, Faithful in participating at church, Involvement in different ministries, etc.

BRIDGE – As a believer, you are called to serve others, just as you serve people at the dinner table.

VISUAL REINFORCEMENT

- Create a different ambiance than you normally have when members arrive. Try creating a romantic environment with candles and soft music to show how little it takes to change the feeling of a place.
- Give each person one paper towel, one paper napkin, one moist towelette, and one cloth napkin. Discuss that there is an appropriate purpose, and time, to use each one of these elements. In the same way, there is an appropriate time for different elements in the church.
- Have different types of bread. A hard roll, slice of regular bread, loaf of French bread, etc., to illustrate how different people are drawn to slight variations of the same thing.

MEDIA REINFORCEMENTS

- Movie clip – "Cheaper by the Dozen" – Scene 3 beginning at 10:40 with the nightmare breakfast and recovery.
- Movie clip – "Shrek 2" – Scene 4 15:00 to 18:30 Formal dinner place setting, and people not knowing purpose of the courses.

THE TABLE THE TWO-FOLD PURPOSE

TAKE HOME OBJECT

- Place a loaf of bread in front of everyone. Have them each take a piece of the bread with them as a reminder to take the Bread of Life with them as they go.
- Give each person a "to go" box or bag to remind them to take Christ outside of the church to others.
- Allow each person to take a note card and write the two-fold purpose of the church on the card. On one side write, "Build Believers" and on the other side write, "Serve Seekers." This is a reminder that there are two parts to the church's purpose and both can exist at the same time.

LEADER NOTES

Describe the first experience you can remember at church.

First impressions play a major role in shaping opinions. Generally, what you are exposed to first is what you believe to be true. So, if the first experience someone has at church is encountering positive people who encourage and build others up, they will expect that from the next church they attend. On the other hand, if the first experience is bad, other churches have a long way to overcome those impressions.

How comfortable are you today at God's Table? What role do you think knowing the purpose of the pieces in the church play in your comfort level?

Understanding the purpose can have a comforting effect. For example, if you have no real concept of what a rollercoaster is and you get on to ride for the first time, the drops, dips, and turns can be nerve-wracking. But, if you know a rollercoaster is designed to thrill you, the actions are more easily welcomed.

It is similar in the church. If you know the biblical blessing behind tithing, you will not be uncomfortable when the offering is collected. If you understand the privilege of prayer, moments of silence in prayer during a service will not be awkward. The knowledge of the purpose goes a long way in causing comfort or discomfort.

Identify the relationship between Christ and the church as described in Ephesians, and come up with other metaphors to help understand this relationship.

Christ is described as the head and the church is described as the body. The key is to identify Christ as the source of direction, plans, guidance, and more. In other words, Christ is the brain. Other metaphors might be: coach and team, steering wheel and car, processor and computer, etc...

Based on the devotionals from this past week, as well as other things you know about Christ, what are examples of how he built up those who believed in him?

One way Christ built up those who believed in him can be seen when we study his relationship with the disciples. Two specific examples listed in the devotionals

125

indicated specific teaching moments. In Mark 9:35-37, Jesus used a child in an illustration of how those who want to be important must serve others. Christ's point was that there is no one too young or lowly to be served by the disciples. Jesus later backed this teaching up when he demonstrated servanthood by washing the disciples' feet (John 13:2-5).

What are examples of how Christ served those seeking him?

The Gospels are full of examples of Christ serving those who seek him. There are numerous healings where those who sought Jesus were served by him. In Matthew 9, we read about Jesus having dinner with the people considered the most sinful of the time. Also, Jesus sent out 72 disciples at one point to go to the surrounding area and teach those who did not know about Christ (Luke 10:1-2).

As a believer, what do you need to be built up?

Different people will emphasize different needs, but there are some things that are common needs for all believers. These needs are so universal, in fact, that they are found in the earliest church. The first church is described as devoting themselves to, "the apostles' teaching and to the fellowship, to the breaking of bread and to prayer" (Acts 2:42). The apostles' teaching is the equivalent to the Bible today. The early believers were committed to obeying God's Word.

The fellowship and breaking of bread are acts of community. These believers were committed to living in a community with other believers. Today, it might be said that they were plugged in to their local church.

Finally, they were dedicated to prayer. They knew the need of communication with God and exercised that privilege.

How has the local church met your needs and built you up?

If you look at the basic needs described in the previous question, most churches revolve their ministries around those needs. Worship services give opportunities for all three previously mentioned needs. Small groups do the same. There are volunteer opportunities to exercise what is learned from God's Word as well as build relationships. The church is full of opportunities to help build up believers.

What could be some of the problems with a church that only builds believers?

First and foremost, the church would be disobedient by not accurately reflecting Christ's purpose. From a practical standpoint, the church would eventually die out. If nobody new is coming in, those who are already a part of the church will eventually move or pass away, leaving the church empty. Also, believers would not grow as Christ intended through sharing him with others. Finally, there would be a lack of fulfillment from only living out part of God's plan. In general, the church would be incomplete.

What were some of the things you were looking for as you were seeking Christ?

The pursuit of peace or purpose in a difficult circumstance can draw some to ask questions about Christ. A major life change such as getting married or having children can cause an adjustment in priorities and a desire for the benefits of being involved in a church. Some people come to church looking for relationships. Others are just curious and looking for answers. These are just a few of the many things that bring people to church.

What did the church offer that helped you find Jesus?

The church should be a place where those who are seeking Christ are welcome. It is the perfect place to come and get questions answered. It is important for members of the church to remember how the church helped them find a relationship with Jesus. This helps them remain open to doing what it takes to help others find a relationship with Jesus. If a member forgets the needs they had, they will be less likely to offer what others need.

What do you think could happen to a church if it was only about serving seekers?

If a church was just about serving seekers, it would once again miss the blessing of being obedient to all God intended for the church. If the focus is on just serving seekers, the members might remain immature and unhealthy. Also, this could lead to making compromises in what the Bible teaches just to make the gospel easier and less offensive in some circles.

What can you do to ensure the ultimate food gets the ultimate presentation at the Table?

One of the keys is to make sure the church is balanced in serving seekers and building believers. If the individuals remember this two-fold purpose and seek to help it exist in the church, the church will stay balanced. When church members forget the purpose of the church and start inserting their own desires for the church, the church is in trouble. Remind yourself of the two-fold purpose on a regular basis and seek ways to support the church in its purpose.

THE CHAIRS

CREATIVE NOTES

ICEBREAKERS:

Idea – "Q&A"

QUESTION – Ask a question that will engage the group and provide a natural lead-in to the rest of your discussion. Those questions might be something like:

- Who was a teacher who helped and inspired you the most?
- What was it about that teacher that helped you grow?
- What was your favorite dish as a child?
- What is your favorite dish now?

BRIDGE – We are influenced by others as we grow up. These people play key roles in helping us mature mentally, physically and spiritually. Also, as we mature our tastes change. Some foods are more commonly liked by mature adults than by children. The same is true in the church. Tastes change as you grow spiritually.

HANDS-ON ACTIVITY

Activity – Popsicle Chair

GUIDELINES/INSTRUCTIONS – Build chairs out of Popsicle sticks and glue.

BRIDGE – These chairs remind us that we all have a chair at The Table.

Activity – Musical Chairs

GUIDELINES/INSTRUCTIONS – Play musical chairs stopping with only three chairs left.

BRIDGE – Everyone fits into one of the three different chairs at the church. Each chair represents a different group: mature believers, new believers, seekers.

Activity – Bringing to the Table

GUIDELINES/INSTRUCTIONS – Divide into three groups and have each group make a collage or draw a picture. Each group will represent one of the following categories: mature believers, new believers, seekers. The pictures and collages should represent what each group brings to The Table.

BRIDGE – Each group brings something different and valuable to The Table.

VISUAL REINFORCEMENTS

- Show a "food pyramid." Explain how the different elements contribute to a balanced diet. Then, talk about how having each of the chairs filled contributes to a balanced church.
- Make a "book cover" that says in large letters: "Recipe Book," and then place it on your Bible before your small group meeting. Explain how the Bible gives you the recipe for a successful meal.
- Place a chair or small table in the center of the group. Place a Bible on it, then add more books: devotional books, religious books, study guides, commentaries, reference books, etc. Discuss if it is possible to gorge ourselves with too much good stuff and eventually become spiritually obese.

MEDIA REINFORCEMENTS

- Movie clip – "Cheaper by the Dozen" – Scene 12 39:11 - 41:56 Shows the rudeness people can have at the table when they are only concerned about themselves.
- Movie clip – "Elf" – Scene 9 43:16 – 44:42 – Demonstration of a bad diet.
- Song – "If We are the Body" by Casting Crowns.

TAKE HOME OBJECTS

- Give each person a baby bottle with 1 Peter 2:1-3 written on it.
- Hand out a formal place card with no name on it reminding them there is a place for everyone at the Table. Have them write someone's name on that card that they want to come to church with them.

LEADER NOTES

How often do you think about your pastors and pray for them?

This question is not designed to produce conviction about not praying for pastors. The goal of this question is to spark the idea that praying for the pastors of your church is significant. It is often overlooked, so you might follow up with the question of "For those of you who pray for your pastors on a regular basis, why?" or "If you do not pray for your pastors regularly, why not?"

How does it make you feel to realize you can play a significant role in the meal by praying for the pastors?

Ephesians 6:19 is preceded by a description of what is commonly called the "armor of God." The author, Paul, is being held captive by the Romans as he awaits trial. It is likely that Paul is looking at a Roman soldier while he was writing Ephesians. Paul relates each piece of the Roman soldier's armor to a piece of spiritual armor. He then starts writing about the importance of prayer. Paul viewed prayer as part of the weaponry God has given believers.

All the other pieces of armor and weapons were for the individual's protection. Paul introduces prayer as a way believers could work together in spiritual battles. It is possible that Paul is still thinking about the Roman soldier and how Roman soldiers strategically worked together in battles. The soldiers lined up in specific formations to defend each other as well as make the strongest offensive strikes. By praying for other believers, you are strategically working together with those believers in the battle between God and Satan.

In praying for your pastors, it is as if you are lining up in a specific battle formation with them to help create a stronger defense, as well as help them reach out. One of the keys to Rome's military success was their strength together. God designed those in the church to be strong by working together.

What are some of the things you think are important to pray on a regular basis for your pastor?

Zechariah 13:7 says, "Strike the shepherd, and the sheep will be scattered...." Satan is aware of this and understands that if he can cause the pastor to have a moral failure or spiritual slip up, it will affect more people than just striking the average person in the church. Because of this, Satan is constantly striking at the pastor by attacking those things that are most important. Common areas of attack are family, friendships and finances. These are all great areas to begin your prayers for the pastor. Pray for the protection of the leaders in your church from temptations. Also, pray for the success of the church as a whole. These are just a few of the prayer needs common to every church.

Why do you think it can be so tempting for Christ followers to become diet driven?

Being diet driven is being focused on yourself. It is the temptation to exclude others and focus on what you need. Every believer is tempted to focus on his or her own life ahead of others. That is why Jesus so strongly emphasized the need to serve others. Jesus knew the drive to turn inward would attack every believer, and the only way to fight it is to get out and serve others.

Share some ways you have been fed by serving others?

Think of food as fuel. Jesus was fueled by accomplishing what God wanted Him to accomplish. Jesus set the example of service, and when you follow in His footsteps you will be fueled as well. There are the practical feelings of accomplishment from serving. There is something very tangible to helping someone in need. There is also the discovery of new things about yourself when your serve others. It seems that those serving always get more out of it than those being served.

Think about your life as a new believer. What helped you get pure spiritual milk to grow?

Most believers can think about a particular person who helped them begin to really understand their relationship with God. That person might be a friend, a volunteer in the church, or any number of other people. Also, being involved in a group of believers where you can ask questions and discuss spiritual issues is important. That allows new believers to get answers they can trust from other believers.

What advice can you offer those who are trying to find a place to serve?

If someone gives you some good advice, share that with others in your group. Help them understand that everyone has unique abilities that can be used in the church. It is important to think about what you like to do and what you do that commonly results in success. Once you have identified that, think about how that could translate into the church. If you really enjoy making people feel welcomed and comfortable, maybe a part of the hospitality ministry is a good fit. If you are good at organizing, consider ushering or parking.

What situations has God placed you in where you can be an appealing aroma to others?

Everywhere you go you can be an appealing aroma. While that is the correct answer, help the group think about specific situations. If you are looking for opportunities to be an appealing aroma, you will find more. For example, instead of stopping at the same gas station each week and paying at the pump, go in and pay the cashier. When you are paying, develop a relationship with the cashier, because chances are you will see them again next week. Instead of just knowing the names of your neighbors, take time to get to know them. Initiate conversations with them, and get to know more about them than how their lawn is doing. The opportunities are out there if you will take the time to look for them.

PUTTING THE PIECES TOGETHER

CREATIVE NOTES

ICEBREAKERS:

Idea – "Q&A"

QUESTION – Ask questions that will engage the group and provide a natural lead-in to the rest of your discussion. Those questions might be something like:

- What scent best describes your personality: cinnamon, lavender, onion, pine tree, gasoline or old spice?
- What is the name of the first cologne or perfume you used?
- What smells remind you of home?

BRIDGE – You can be recognized by your scent. Some smells immediately produce emotions from previous experiences. The church should give off an attractive aroma, because it represents Christ.

Idea – Show and Tell

ACTIVITY – Divide the group into teams of two to three. Give each group a common household object such as a hair brush, wire whisk, screwdriver, etc. Allow them a few minutes to come up with a presentation to sell their object to the group. Let each group present and then vote on who had the best presentation.

BRIDGE – The presentation can make a significant difference. When time is put into the presentation, it can make you think about the object in new way. Presentation is also important in the church.

Idea – Deserted Dessert

ILLUSTRATION – Prepare a dessert to be specifically served while everyone is sitting around during the icebreaker. Leave an important ingredient out of the dessert, such as sugar. Watch the reactions of the others as they taste it for the first time. After they have tried the dessert, let them know you left an ingredient out and have them discuss the effect on the dessert.

BRIDGE – Each and every ingredient is important in a recipe. The same is true in the church.

HANDS-ON ACTIVITY

Activity – Puzzled

INSTRUCTIONS/GUIDELINES – Bring a small puzzle to the group (ideally 25 pieces or less). Before anyone arrives, remove several pieces from the puzzle. Let the group try to put the puzzle together.

BRIDGE – A few missing pieces can make a significant difference in the final picture of the puzzle. Missing pieces in the church can contribute to skewing the big picture of God.

Activity – Puzzle Pace

INSTRUCTIONS/GUIDELINES – Divide into groups of three to four. Let each group take turns trying to put together a small puzzle as quickly as they can. A good size puzzle is a preschool puzzle with 10 pieces. The goal is to be the group who puts the puzzle together the fastest.

BRIDGE – The team can play a significant part in putting together the big picture. In the church, everyone works together to display God's big picture.

Activity – Series Charades

- Write titles of previous messages or series at your church on small pieces of paper and put them in a hat. Divide into two teams and take turns choosing the titles and trying to act them out.

  For example, here are some previous series titles we've done at Fellowship: Love Affair, Authority Issues, Thread, Retro, In The Zone, The Table, Questions, Who's Kidding Who, Decoding the DaVinci Code, RPM's (Recognizing Potential Mates), Forgiveness – The Real F Word.

VISUAL REINFORCEMENT

- Place a properly prepared dish in front of everyone with a nice garnish and presentation. Beside it, place another dish that is burned and ruined. Think about

how the presentation makes an important difference.
- Have a movie clap board that says "Action" with 1 Peter 2:9-12 written on it.
- Display a movie poster or an ad with key information cut out. It displays the importance different pieces can play.

MEDIA REINFORCEMENTS

- Movie clip – "Hitch" – Scene 7 from 28:21 – 29:40 This clip shows creative approaches to presentation.
- Movie clip – "Hitch" – Scene 1 from the start to 2:48 Demonstrates how to create opportunities to get noticed.

TAKE HOME OBJECT

- Hand out puzzle pieces to remind each person they contribute to the big picture at church.
- Have volunteer applications ready so anyone wanting to contribute to the church can see the options available.
- Hand out chain links to represent the connection each Christ follower has, not only to their current church, but all the way back the very first church.
- Pass out generic invitations and encourage each person to write the name of someone they would like to invite to church. Then, place the invitations somewhere prominent to serve as a reminder to invite that person.

LEADER NOTES

What are some of the phrases used to describe Christ followers in these verses and explain what you think they mean?

The following are the phrases: "chosen people," "royal priesthood," "holy nation," "people belonging to God," "people of God," "friends," "aliens" and "strangers."

The theme throughout most of these phrases is a special group. The church is a special group of people intimately connected to God in a way those outside the church are not connected.

There is an interesting connection between what Peter wrote in these verses and what is written in Exodus 19:5-6. "Now if you obey me fully and keep my covenant, then out of all nations you will be my treasured possession. Although the whole earth is mine, you will be for me a kingdom of priests and a holy nation.' These are the words you are to speak to the Israelites."

This was the promise given to Moses shortly after God rescued Israel from slavery in

Egypt. God has rescued those who follow Christ from the slavery of sin, so they have the opportunity to become God's people.

As Christ followers, what actions are we called to take?

The following are the actions listed: abstain from sinful desires, live...good lives.

A good follow up question is, "What is the relationship between these actions and who you are in Christ as described in these verses?"

What can the response of non-believers be when we follow Christ?

When those outside the church see you living out who God has made you in Christ, they will notice something different about you. At first, it might cause anger or resentment. You have probably all experienced someone accusing you of judging them because you do not live the way they choose to live. Your life of love will stand out. You do not have to drive a special type of car or wear special shirts with Christian logos to make you stand out. Your life of love will stand out. Once those around you experience your love, they may still resist, but they will eventually give God glory.

What have been some of the most creative and compelling elements you have seen at church?

Think through all the things you have seen happen at the church. It could be the way a particular person serves at the church that moved you the most. Songs have a powerful impact because they often articulate thoughts and feelings in unique ways. Illustrations in messages can last in someone's mind far beyond the rest of the message. Whatever the element, encourage the person to explain why that element is so significant to them.

How have those you invited to the Table responded to the elements?

It is important to remember how God has used the church to impact those you know. If you lose track of how God is impacting others, you will not appreciate all that is happening at the church. It is also important to remember the impact to encourage you to continue inviting others and give them the opportunity to be impacted.

Try to brainstorm all the volunteer positions happening on a weekend and how each position contributes to the presentation.

The list is long. While you are brainstorming, try to get specific with positions so you do not miss how many opportunities there actually are. For example, there are numerous positions in children's ministry. There are teachers from the stage, small group leaders, volunteers who run the audio and video, greeters, and check-in volunteers. This allows the group to realize how much work goes into a weekend. Also, it emphasizes the importance of everyone using his or her unique abilities in the church for the overall purpose of the church. If anyone is not using their abilities, the church is missing out.

THE TABLE

To you, what is the most incredible part of the church?

The church is an amazing example of how people from diverse backgrounds with conflicting interests can develop intimate relationships. Wounds that have afflicted people for years find healing. Marriages that were quickly dissolving find strength. Lonely individuals find love in healthy ways. People get invited to participate in a life they may have previously thought impossible. There are many reasons the church is incredible. Use this opportunity to remind each other of all the incredible parts of the church.

CHECK OUT THESE OTHER STUDIES BY ED YOUNG COMING SOON TO CREATIVEPASTORS.COM:

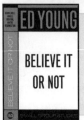

Believe It or Not
What The Bible Says About Heaven, Hell, Angels, Creation, And The Resurrection
Do you believe everything you read...or not? When it comes to the claims of the Bible, you have to ask yourself the same question: Do you believe it or not?

Juicy Fruit
Living Life In The Spirit
Learn what it means to produce spiritual fruit and to personally develop characteristics of the Christian life in this in-depth, five-week study on the fruit of the Spirit.

Know Fear
Facing Life's Phobias
Facing life's common fears with uncommon faith can make all the difference between happiness and a life of terror. Ed Young, in this creative study, gives solid Biblical solutions allowing you to know fear in a life-changing way.

The Creative Marriage
The Art Of Keeping Your Love Alive
Disposable relationships and throw-away marriages permeate our culture. When the dream fades and the realities of life set in, many just throw in the towel. In this six-week study, Ed speaks openly and honestly about the hard work involved in a creative marriage and the lasting rewards of doing it God's way.

In The Zone
Living In The Sweet Spot Of God's Success
Do you want to live a life in marked contrast to those around you? In this study, Ed Young shares powerful biblical principles about what it means to live a life blessed by God—to live *in the zone*.

Snapshots of the Savior
Jesus—Up Close And Personal
So often when we think of Jesus' life, our photo album is limited and sketchy. In this powerful study of talks, Ed Young shares vivid images from the Bible to help provide a broader, panoramic view of Christ's mission and ministry.

*Studies on this page are available at quantity discounts.

Mission Possible

Everyday Leadership Principles For Everyday People

With an impossible mission before him, Nehemiah allowed God to develop him as a leader and to give him the skills and character necessary to carry out his mission successfully. This study uncovers the timeless leadership principles found in this Old Testament power struggle between conniving political leaders and a persevering construction mogul.

X-Trials – Takin' Life to the X-Treme

An Extreme Study In The Book Of James

In this book, X-Trials, Ed Young leads you through a verse-by-verse look at one of the most challenging and controversial books of the Bible, the book of James. Living life as a Christ-follower in today's world requires extreme faith!

Character Tour

A Biblical Tour Of Some Great Characters With Great Character

Certain character qualities stand out in notable characters throughout the Bible. In this creative series, Ed Young uses those great biblical role models to help us crack the character code and become people who live out godly character from the inside out.

Virtuous Reality

The Relationships Of David

People in your life can pull you up or drag you down. Join this journey into the life of David as we discover how this "man after God's own heart" lived out the daily reality of his relationships. By uncovering the good and bad in your relationships, Ed Young will help you discover how to honor God regardless of who crosses your path.

Ignite

Refining And Purifying Your Faith

Fire, it is a source of destruction and a source of life. It incinerates and destroys. But it also refines and purifies. In the Bible, God used fire and other trials to turn up the heat and reveal His power through the lives of people. Ed Young explores these trials from Scripture to help fan the flames of our own faith today.

Tri-GOD

Understanding The Trinity

Three in One, One in Three. The Trinity. God in three persons--Father, Son, and Holy Spirit--is one of the most misunderstood doctrines in the Christian church. Yet Ed Young teaches in this exciting new series that our awareness of God's triune nature is pivotal to growing with Him.

First and 10
The Whats, Whys And Hows Of The Ten Commandments

Where do we find our moral foundation in this game of life? In a world of ever-changing culture, circumstances, and philosophies it all goes back to the big ten. Ed Young will take you on a thought-provoking, soul-searching look at the Ten Commandments.

Wired for Worship
Make Worship A Part Of Your Every Day Life

There is great debate and misconception surrounding "worship." One thing holds true, as human beings we are wired for worship. Whether it is career and finances or relationships and family, we instinctively worship something. Join Ed Young as he dives in to discover what it means to truly worship God in your life.

Praying for Keeps
A Guide To Prayer

Imagine how awesome it would be to sit down and have a face-to-face conversation with God! In the small-group study, you will learn how you can effectively and naturally communicate with God. Ed Young will walk you through the biblical principles that will guide you into a more intimate and rewarding life of prayer.

Fatal Distractions
Avoid The Downward Spiral Of Sin

In this in-depth study, Pastor Ed Young makes a frontal assault on the seven deadly sins that threaten to destroy our lives.

Marriage Unveiled
Components Of A Healthy, Vibrant Marriage

This dynamic study uncovers the essential elements that will keep you growing together for a lifetime. Through this straight-forward, no-holds-barred approach, you will experience help and hope for troubled marriages as well as a challenge to make great marriages greater.

RPMs - Recognizing Potential Mates
Supercharge Your Dating Life

Whether you're a single adult, a student, or a parent, this creatively driven study will provide foundational principles on how to date and select a mate God's way. We're going to cruise past the cultural myths and embark on a supercharged ride to the ultimate relational destination.